LITTLE FIGHTERS

The Million-to-One Miracles

LITTLE FIGHTERS

The Million-to-One Miracles

**ANGIE BENHAFFAF
WITH EDEL O'CONNELL** ～

Gill & Macmillan

Gill & Macmillan Ltd
Hume Avenue, Park West, Dublin 12
with associated companies throughout the world
www.gillmacmillan.ie

© Angie Benhaffaf 2011
978 07171 5009 0

Typography design by Make Communication
Print origination by Síofra Murphy
Printed and bound in the UK by MPG Books Ltd, Cornwall

This book is typeset in Minion 13/16 pt.

The paper used in this book comes from the wood pulp of
managed forests. For every tree felled, at least one tree is
planted, thereby renewing natural resources.

A CIP catalogue record for this book is available from the
British Library.

5 4 3 2 1

CONTENTS

I would like to dedicate this book to my four beautiful children. I am honoured to be your Mum and I thank you for bringing so much happiness into my life.

Malika, you have given me love and affection at times I needed it most.

Iman, you gave me strength and humour in the most difficult, sad situations.

Hassan and Hussein, you have given me courage and faith, and reminded us all that 'miracles still happen, and dreams do come true'.

My wonderful husband Azzedine, I told you at the very start that they were 'Little Fighters', just like their Daddy.

I would like this book to keep alive the memory of a 'special' little angel that left her loving family in 2010.

Léana Martin, 'a beautiful light in the lives of all she touched', 29 November 2002–29 October 2010.

Chapter 1 ∽

| LIFE-CHANGING NEWS

'I'm really worried about this scan,' I confessed to the pleasant-faced sonographer as I lay back on a clinical hospital bed anticipating the sudden freeze of cold gel. I tried to ignore the gathering dread in my stomach as my two-year-old daughter, Iman, chatted to herself beside me in her pushchair. I had longed for this, my third child, and today I was to see my baby for the first time. I had done everything I could to promote a healthy pregnancy, but I couldn't help feeling that something was very wrong. I shifted nervously on the bed as the placid sonographer smiled at me reassuringly and switched on the monitor. I closed my eyes for a moment as she traced the probe over the swell of my belly. I was afraid to breathe. Then it came, that terrible moment when I watched her expression slowly darken as a creeping, cold sweat inched its way down my spine. I could hear her trying to control the growing panic in her voice as she whispered, 'I'm seeing something here I've never seen before,' the colour draining from her face. 'Your babies . . . they are joined.'

Those unimaginable words were to change my life forever.

I met my husband Azzedine in a hotel in Rathmines in March 1997. The first time I saw him it felt as if a thunderbolt had hit me. As soon as our eyes met there was this instant connection that seemed ancient. Azzedine, being Muslim, and from Algeria, insisted on quite a formal courtship; sometimes, when I was with him, it felt as if time had somehow wound back to a quieter, simpler age. He was sweet and protective, and so completely different from anyone I had ever met. I remember him cooking dinner for me in my Dublin apartment, and us spending hours discussing our hopes for the future, and those unborn babies we were yet to meet. Azzedine looked after me, but in many ways I looked after him too. Growing up in Algeria, he had seen some unspeakable things, and these haunted him, haunted his dreams, but I knew we could build a happy life together. We were together only a short few months before we began to talk about having children, and it was clear we both wanted them very much. I knew we would make great parents so, two and a half years later, in September 1999, we were married. It was a gorgeous day, the fairytale ending I had always dreamed of for us.

We moved to my homeplace, Cork, to build a life together and worked hard for the next number of years saving for that coveted mortgage deposit, before starting a family. Azzedine, a chef, worked long, crucifying hours without complaint, and I worked as a receptionist with Bowen Construction. I loved my job, but after my first child, Malika, was born in 2005 I knew I wanted to be with her all the time. Malika was two weeks overdue. When she finally arrived I could hardly believe how amazing she was; her tiny little body knew me instinctively, and I, like most Mums, felt I had finally done what I had been put on this earth to do. I remember the happiness we felt with our newborn. I knew I couldn't leave her with a stranger, so, after much soul searching, I decided to hand in my notice and become a full-time mother. I loved being a Mum more than anything so two years later, on 17 June 2007, we had a second little girl, Iman. She was such an angelic child, delicate like a china doll. I adored her. We spent every waking minute together as a family; we went everywhere together, and were happiest in each other's company.

When Iman was two years old we began to think about having a third child. I had always really enjoyed the time when the children were small, the newness of them, the smell of them. I knew Azzedine longed for a boy and, if I was honest, part of me did too. Both Malika and Iman were very girly, with their big brown eyes and their fairy-princess dresses. I pictured Azzedine playing football with our handsome son, a miniature version of himself, and so, quietly, I hoped. We tried for a while, and I recall the gut-wrenching disappointment of negative pregnancy tests, but then, one bright and glorious Saturday afternoon, I discovered I was pregnant again. I remember the sweet rush of happiness at seeing that welcome blue line. I was unable to conceal this wonderful news so my father excitedly bundled me and the two girls into the car and headed straight for the Bosun Restaurant in Monkstown, Co. Cork, where Azzedine worked. I felt like a giddy teenager on that gorgeous summer's day; I couldn't wait to give him the good news.

I had always loved being pregnant. I loved everything about it—the growing swell of my tummy, the cravings, feeling that life grow inside me. I relished the hustle and bustle leading up to having the baby, and finally the quiet joy of bringing that tiny bundle home, full of expectation and promise. I could never put a number on the babies we might have, and I always imagined a large gang of raggle-taggle kids around us. I could think of nothing more perfect than growing old together with all of our children and grandchildren by our sides.

Finally, I saw the sign for Monkstown, and as my excitement grew we pulled up outside the restaurant. I called Azzedine on his mobile and begged him to come out, just for a moment. Saturday evening was the busiest night of the week for him, so it was not easy, but eventually he managed to sneak away. Almost as soon as he approached the car, I showed him the pregnancy stick. We were like teenagers embracing and laughing in the sunlight; it was such a wonderful moment. Everything felt so light—so full of hope and possibility. As I pulled away Azzedine jokingly shouted after me, 'If this is another girl, I'm going back to my mother!', a peal of laughter coming from his open mouth and the tiny dream of our new baby beginning to nestle in our hearts. This was to be one of our last happy days.

I can remember the first time I began to feel unsettled about my pregnancy. I had taken the pregnancy test out of the bathroom cabinet to put it with the other mementoes I had been keeping for my children when I accidentally dropped it. My heart sank as it crashed onto the tiled floor of the bathroom. When I bent to pick it up I noticed the positive sign had turned to a negative. Try as I might, I couldn't get it to change. I knew it was irrational and silly, but it unsettled me. Physically, I also felt very different with this pregnancy: I felt unwell and tired, and not as full of life as I had done with the girls. I dismissed this as possibly being down to the baby being a different sex, but for some reason worry began to grow even as my baby formed inside me. I recall telling a close friend, Alex, how I was absolutely terrified to go for my first scan; I had a feeling something was wrong this time. I fought back tears as I confided in her one lovely afternoon while our carefree children chased each other through the trees. She did her best to reassure me, just putting it down to nerves, and we dropped the subject, but still this niggling feeling bothered me for the first few months. During my previous two pregnancies I had been excited about the initial scans. I would go into them full of positivity, confident in the expectation that I would see this perfectly forming foetus on the screen, after which I expected to go home with my wonderful, if a little indecipherable, scan. Now I know that when it comes to your pregnancy, you can't take anything for granted.

———

My first, 12-week, scan fell on a hot July day. I vividly recall everything about the afternoon that changed our lives irrevocably. There we were, all four of us, in the waiting room of Cork University Maternity Hospital (CUMH) excitedly anticipating seeing the latest addition to our little family. I remember such minutiae about it: half-heartedly watching the 'Ellen' talk show on the scratchy waiting room TV; Azzedine going up and down to the water tank constantly refilling my plastic cup, as my drinking a lot of water would mean we would get a perfectly clear image of the new baby. I had brought little bags of sweets for the children to keep them quiet and, as we waited, butterflies fluttered in my stomach. Finally, it came to our turn; we were about to get our first glimpse of bump number three! I never smoked, I don't drink, and I had taken my folic acid, so I knew that there should be nothing to worry about, but still this niggling worry-worm gnawed at me from inside. Just as my name was called, Malika said she needed to use the bathroom. I was nervous to go in without Azzedine. I really didn't want him to miss anything, but he reassured me he would not be long, so I went into that awful room with two-year-old Iman in her pushchair.

A pleasant sonographer, who introduced herself as Kate, told me to lie back on the bed so she could begin to prepare me. I remember the cold gel on my tummy, and the expectation of it all. I really wanted to wait for Azzedine to come back in, but the sonographer said we should go right ahead and get started, so I nodded in agreement. I told her I had felt quite frightened for weeks about what the scan would reveal. She looked at me, confused. I wasn't really sure why, but I just had this ominous feeling I could not shake. Smiling at me, she reassured me everything would be OK, that it was just nerves. She flipped the switch on the monitor and reached towards my belly with the probe of the scanner.

I recall that all-seeing eye sweeping along the length of my belly and within seconds I knew something was very wrong. Even now,

I'm back there, in that hateful room, watching her face completely drain of colour, the sudden look of distress, the confusion at what she saw. 'What's wrong with my baby?' I demanded, growing increasingly alarmed. At first she wouldn't tell me, she said she wanted to wait for Azzedine to come in, but I pleaded with her. 'Please!' I half yelled, 'you have to tell me now. I can't wait. What is wrong with my baby?' She could hear the rising panic in my voice. 'Is it dead?' I shouted in disbelief, at the suddenness of the situation. My mind began to race. I tried to imagine all the possibilities, the worst being that the baby had died inside me; there was no heartbeat, no life. Then suddenly she said, 'No, no, it's not that. I am seeing twins here,' still sounding strange and uneasy. At first I was overjoyed; I thought perhaps she had just looked worried because she hadn't expected to see two babies. 'But that is just fantastic!' I told her, my poor heart skipping with joy for that one fleeting, blissful moment. 'Twins'—even the sound of the word made me think of matching babygrows, bottles and two little cherubic heads, but I could see her expression hadn't changed.

I could tell she was about to say something I really didn't want to hear. I wanted to throw my hands over my ears and run out of there. 'I'm very sorry to tell you this,' she said, her face flooding with sympathy, 'but I am seeing something here I have never seen before. Your babies . . . they are joined.' The words seemed to hang in the air for a moment as if a firework had gone off and traces of it still remained, suspended, lifeless. The room began to spin at a nauseating pace. I held on to the sides of the bed for support. My mind was attempting to grasp what had just been said to me, but terror had a grip around my throat, choking me. A roaring darkness rushed towards me in the stillness. I felt as if I were in someone else's terrifying nightmare, watching it, frozen, liminal. I could hear the sonographer say something about wanting to find an obstetrician. 'What I am seeing on this scan I have never seen before,' she said. 'I am really going to have to get a second opinion.' Her disembodied voice seemed to echo in my head. In the space of a few minutes our lives had been turned upside-down. Everyone had been so excited in the waiting room, and now I was desperate to crawl on my knees back to that moment before the monitor was turned on and revealed our broken dreams.

Just then Azzedine walked into the room with Malika; he strolled into complete chaos. He opened the door to find his little girl screaming in terror, his wife wailing, and a look of despair on the sonographer's face. I had my knees pulled right up to my chest as this crushing news throbbed relentlessly in my head. He immediately started to panic and repeat over and over, 'What's wrong? What's wrong?' I couldn't see the screen, because a fog had come down over everything; neither could I see through my hot tears. I had never cried like that in my whole life; it was a low, wailing sound, a mother grieving for her unborn children. I felt my heart actually break. 'The babies, the babies are joined!' I shouted at my terrified husband, the words like shards of glass on my tongue. I could tell he didn't take this in, did not want to understand. I wished I could travel back through time to silence those words and never hear them again, but I knew I never could.

The sonographer asked us to wait, and left the room. I remember the pain at seeing Malika burst into tears, while Iman wailed and wailed in her pushchair. I just held on to my husband in terror. I tried to tell him what was going on. I had watched documentaries about conjoined twins in the past, so I knew what it meant. I knew the word more associated with them was 'Siamese', a word I grew to hate; even the sound of it on my tongue makes me sick.

For what seemed like an eternity we waited in that dark room—it must have been up to an hour—with this hideous truth between us as if a thief had crept into our lives amid the gloom, stealing our hopes, drowning our happiness. My bladder was so full, having drunk so much water, that it began to ache; I left to find a toilet. I remember trying to pull myself together in the bathroom and catching a glimpse of my horrified, pale face and puffy eyes. I begged God to please, please let the doctors be wrong. I longed for someone to tell me it had all been a giant error; that they had looked at the scan again and everything was OK.

I went back to my frightened little girls; all I wanted to do was bundle their little bodies together and run out of that place. I had to take Iman out of her buggy to breastfeed her amid all that madness and I remember how even this simple act of mothering made my broken heart ache. It seemed so natural, and yet there, on the screen, was this inescapable image of our future. As I fed one child I was also mourning for the two I feared I might never mother.

With Iman calmed, I tried to reassure Malika, so I just told her we were sad because something was wrong with one of the babies. We had always tried to be as honest as possible with the children, but it was hard to see her scared little face. Eventually, after what seemed like hours, the sonographer arrived back with an obstetrician, Dr Keelin O'Donoghue. I was comforted that it was a woman and, although she did her best to reassure me, as soon as she started to scan again she immediately saw the babies were joined; there was absolutely no doubt. She looked me straight in the face and told me they were joined from the chest down, and it was likely they shared a heart and all the vital organs. She also told me there was a strong possibility that both babies could die. 'Both babies could die'—how a mother is ever expected to take these words and allow them in I will never understand. I was then given even more shattering news: if the babies didn't die, and I went full-term, my own life would be at risk during the delivery, and I also faced the risk of a hysterectomy. This latest information was like a tsunami of pain crashing over me; none of it was really sinking it. The obstetrician told us we could go home, but we would have to come back the following Tuesday, and indeed once a week from that point forward for more scans. I just sat there with this knowledge and felt it seep into me like a poison. Mechanically, I texted my father and asked him to come to the hospital, so I could tell him what had happened. They let him into the darkened scan room; the news absolutely devastated him. I really didn't want to leave the hospital that day, didn't want to walk out those doors and bring that awful truth into my life, into our home, into our hearts.

We drove home in silence. I went into the house, closed the front door, pulled down the wooden shutters and headed straight for the living room, where I slowly died inside. I stared for hours at the scanned image of my sons, the perfect love-heart shape their little bodies made. I couldn't eat; I couldn't drink; I didn't want to see anyone, talk to anyone. All I did was sit on the sofa as the clock ticked and I sobbed uncontrollably. My face hurt, my heart ached with sadness and my head pounded. I remember Malika coming in and out and rubbing my head, or bringing down a pillow or one of her blankets to put over me, and it broke my heart all over again. Azzedine was absolutely devastated, but had to return to work the very next day. I know it killed him to leave me, but what could he do? I spent many days alone with that truth, endless days running into nights with those two precious little girls like watchful ghosts. It may have been summer outside, but it was winter in our home.

I dreaded returning to the hospital; the place I had previously associated with the happy birth of my healthy little girl Iman had now become a looming vision of hell, a prison from which I could not escape my own crushing truth. The sheer agony of having to walk back through those doors was unbearable. We knew we couldn't do this alone, so I asked my father to call his sister Val to see if she would come and care for the girls on Tuesday whilst we returned to the hospital for my next scan. When she first heard I was going for a scan she was thrilled and excited as she had not known I was pregnant. My poor father broke down as he told her the pregnancy didn't look good. Val didn't ask for any more information; she just accepted that help was required. So, the following Tuesday she called to our home with my cousin's wife Sinead. They took one look at me and knew I had been to hell and back. I fell into their arms and told them my terrible news. I dreaded that next scan. Later that day as I walked towards the hospital everything began to swim in front of me, my legs turning to jelly. I was having a panic attack. I remember the look of worry on Azzedine's face as I sat on the ground taking huge, gasping breaths, confusion and pity on the faces of those first-time Dads and happy relatives going in to visit their bright and shiny newborns. I was so weak from not eating that I could barely walk; my lips cracked and bled from dehydration. I never wanted to go into that awful room again and be forced to see an image of my babies' future on that unforgiving screen.

———

Looking back now I know that during those first days I was in denial. I had even managed to convince myself that the sonographer and the obstetrician had got it all wrong. I imagined their apologies and sighs of relief when they turned on the scanner the second time and realised their folly. I desperately tried to tell myself that perhaps they had made a mistake, but in my heart I knew it to be true. My worried father quizzed the doctors and asked them why, if my life was in danger, could they not intervene, but they told us they could get involved only if I presented to the hospital in a serious and life-threatening condition. As she had been present at the first scan, and had heard what had been said, Malika began to believe that if the babies died inside me I would also be lost to her. I remember the anxiety in her little voice as she repeatedly asked me, 'Mummy, if the babies die in your tummy, will you die too?' I tried to reassure her as best I could that the babies were going to live, but it devastated me to see the furrow of worry in her babyish brow.

Despite my own enormous fear, I never contemplated terminating the pregnancy. There was never even a moment that I considered quashing any chance those babies had at life. I remember thinking even if there would be only one little kick, one tiny flutter, I was going to feel it; even if we were going to have those little twins with us for half an hour, I was going to know them; even if we were going to hold them only one precious time, I was going to have that hold. I understood there was a high risk that the babies would either be stillborn or would die within the first 24 hours, but I also knew I was their mother and I was going to fight for them. After all, if I wasn't going to, who would? And, in the end, those little boys fought enough for all of us. From my own research I discovered the survival rate for conjoined twins was very small; that many of those tiny lives that managed to survive a complex and difficult delivery died after 24 hours, so I knew, and Azzedine knew, that this was a one in a million chance, but there was that tiny chance, as tiny as their little bird-beating hearts in the palm of my hand.

Every morning I had to relive the agony and in those blissful moments between sleep and waking I would always forget the babies were joined. I would rub my pregnant belly and feel the joy of life within me and then that deadly wave would come crashing through the windows: the razor-sharp pain of truth. I asked at the hospital whether other parents of conjoined twins would see me, and talk about their experiences, but to no avail. Perhaps the outcomes of their pregnancies had been so torturously bleak they hadn't wanted to open up old wounds again, and I understand that, but it was such a hopeless and lonely time. I felt nobody understood what I was going through, and felt helpless all the time. All light had left my life. The only thing the doctors seemed to know for sure was that my babies might not live; I might never hold them, name them, and they might never call me Mummy. My future seemed to have been stolen from me by this awful truth, and I dreaded each miserable dawn as it brought me closer and closer to what might be.

Chapter 2 ∾

IMAGES OF HOPE

Conjoined twins are identical twins whose bodies are joined in the womb. Approximately 40 to 60 per cent arrive in the world stillborn. They are exceedingly rare, with an incidence of about one in 250,000 live births. They can be joined at the chest, head, abdomen or hip. Approximately 30 per cent of conjoined twins survive only one day. In fact, the overall survival rate of conjoined twins is somewhere between 5 and 25 per cent. For some reason, female siblings seem to have a much greater chance of survival than male twins; almost 75 per cent of all live births of conjoined twins are girls. As they are genetically identical, the twins are always the same sex. They develop from the same fertilised egg, and they share the same amniotic cavity and placenta.

Twins are formed in the womb one of two ways: either a woman releases two eggs instead of the usual one, or she produces only one egg that divides after fertilisation. If she releases two eggs, which are fertilised by separate sperm, she has fraternal twins. However, when a single fertilised egg divides and separates, she has identical or paternal twins. In the case of conjoined twins, a woman produces only a single egg, which does not fully divide after fertilisation. The developing embryo starts to split into identical twins during the first few weeks after conception, but unfortunately stops before the process is completed. The partially separated egg then develops into a conjoined foetus. There is no typical case when it comes to conjoined twins—where the babies are joined, the number and type of organs shared—and how healthy the babies are at birth varies widely.

During those first few weeks of grieving I felt as if I was merely existing rather than living. My GP, Dr Lynda O'Callaghan, called to see me almost every day and was the first of many members of the medical profession whose unbelievable kindness got me through the most difficult year of my life. The day after my second scan I called two of my friends who have children in Malika's class so I could tell them what had happened. Many of the other Mums at Malika's school had been aware I was going for my first scan and knew how excited I was about it. I just couldn't face being asked about it and really wanted a way out of having to discuss my devastating news with them. My friends Joan and Carmel called the next day and when I answered the door they could see from my gaunt face and hollow eyes that something terrible had happened. I told them my babies were joined and might not live; they were speechless. Azzedine was at work and I was alone with the girls so I desperately needed someone to listen and be there for me. They promised they would make sure the other Mums wouldn't ask me any probing questions, for which I was deeply grateful. It felt good just to be able to tell someone that I was carrying conjoined twins, to say those words that had been pressing down on my chest for a week, dragging me under like a diving bell.

I also decided to contact our family GP, Dr Joe Dillon. At a time when I believed I couldn't trust many people with our shocking secret, he was someone I felt I could speak to in confidence. He was the doctor who had cared for me since I was a baby, and I trusted him implicitly. I called him up one day and told him about the babies. Dr Dillon informed me an old college friend of his, working at Great Ormond Street Hospital (GOSH) in London, specialised in the separation of conjoined twins, Mr Edward Kiely. He told me Mr Kiely was a world-leading consultant paediatric surgeon who had been managing conjoined twins at the hospital since the eighties. I couldn't believe this; it seemed as if someone had thrown my drowning hopes a lifeline. Dr Dillon told me to phone the hospital and ask him for advice.

Eventually I plucked up the courage to take the first step. I was extremely nervous as I dialled the number and listened to the droning overseas ringtone. Eventually I managed to get through to his secretary. By chance the man himself walked into his office while I was trying to explain my situation; the next thing I heard was this reassuring voice on the end of the phone. I struggled not to break down as I told him the basic details of how my twins were thought to share all the major organs, including the heart. I pleaded with him to be honest with me as to their chances. I felt my own desperate heart sink as he explained that as the babies shared a heart they had little chance of survival. I could hardly respond to this devastating blow. Before I hung up, Mr Kiely reassured me, and gave me his mobile number and email address just in case I needed anything. I thanked him with the last ounce of composure left in my trembling body, hung up the phone and slid down the wall onto the kitchen floor in tears; this was not what I wanted to hear. My tiny glimmer of hope was flickering and slowly dying.

From that point on I began to fall further and further into a grim place. I had always taken pride in my appearance; now I barely dressed myself in the mornings. I lived in my dressing gown, sloping around the dark house, feeling like a ghost haunting my own corridors. The only time I left home was to attend my weekly scans. I dreaded seeing the babies' image on the screen, dreaded hearing more bad news. I would often ask the sonographer to turn the monitor away from my view, unable to look at my growing boys bound in what then seemed like a deadly embrace. A new sonographer, Marion Cunningham, who specialised in multiple births, took over my care at CUMH, and she, along with my patient obstetrician, Dr Keelin O'Donoghue, watched and waited with us week after week as the babies grew together inside me. They had told me it was usually in the first trimester that conjoined twins were lost, so we just waited, hour by hour, ominous day after ominous day, for that terrible event to occur. I would get a sudden, sharp pain or cramp, and I would think: 'This is it; I'm losing them.' I was walking around with a time bomb in my womb, and I waited for it to go off in my darkened home as the clock ticked on the wall. I was terrified all the time that my babies would slip away.

By this stage September was fast approaching, and it was almost time for Malika to go back to school. All summer long my patient girl had watched her mother fall apart. Her summer holiday had consisted of nothing but pain and sorrow, as the sun slowly set on our family's happiness. I realised the week before she was due to go back to school that she had neither books nor uniform, so I knew I had to get up off the couch and get my little girl ready.

One Saturday afternoon I finally worked up the will to get dressed, put Iman's pushchair in the car, and headed towards Cork City with my girls to do some back-to-school shopping. Our first stop was a Mothercare store on St Patrick's Street. Pregnant and weak, I struggled with the buggy, so I left it unattended for a moment in order to get some shoes for Malika. On my return, I realised with horror that someone had snatched my purse. That was the first time I had been out in public in weeks; it had taken every ounce of my remaining will to leave the house. I knew the ticket for the car park had also been in my purse and I became overwhelmed with grief. I just burst into tears in the store. The Gardaí arrived and I remember telling them through my hysteria that I was pregnant with these babies that were not going to live, that I was in town with my two children and I couldn't get to my car, and I had no money to get home. All the money I had for Malika's things was gone. The Gardaí drove us back to the car park and helped us to get the car out, for which I was extremely grateful, but I felt a debilitating helplessness and frustration. I wanted to scream at the world 'Why me?' When I finally got home I thought to myself: 'I am never leaving this house again.' All I wanted to do was to stay in my cocoon of grief and mourn for my babies, for my family's dreams.

I was booked in for another scan a few days later in Cork with a Dr Orla Franklin, a heart specialist who had been sent down from Dublin to examine the heart the doctors believed my babies shared. When I was first notified of this appointment, it filled me with dread; I was 20 weeks pregnant, and dreading even more horrifying news. We drove up to the hospital in silence, fear tightening its grip around my throat as we neared the sprawling campus. When the scan eventually got underway we braced ourselves for the worst. I said to Dr Franklin, 'Whatever happens today, there is one thing I really want to know, and that is the sex of my babies.' I just wanted to know if the twins were boys or girls, regardless of their shared heart, or their shared organs, or any other unfathomable and distressing medical information we had been given up to that point. These were my babies, and I wanted to know them. I told Dr Franklin that I thought they were little boys. The doctors felt this would be highly unlikely as more than 70 per cent of conjoined twins were female and the survival rate for boys was very low, but in my heart I knew they were little boys: my two Little Fighters. I knew Azzedine and I had been longing for a little boy so much that there was a chance. I had already picked out names for them just in case, and regardless of the outcome I was excited to find out the sex. Azzedine, however, was not thinking along these lines at all; in fact, he feared the twins would be the boys he had longed for so dearly. The very thought of that dream being dangled before him and then cruelly snatched away filled him with despair.

Finally, Dr Franklin turned off the machinery and sat us down to speak to us about her findings. The news she gave us that day was to change everything. The babies did not share a heart; in fact they had one each! It seemed as if a shaft of blinding light had burst through that darkened room and warmed my frozen heart. This meant the twins had, albeit small, a better chance of surviving, and that was probably the best news I had ever heard. But there was more to come. Dr Franklin also told me that I was, in fact, carrying two boys—a revelation that produced in me the sweetest sorrow. I think I experienced the whole spectrum of human emotion simultaneously. I cried as I rubbed the swell of my tummy, and dared to dream that I may someday hold my little boys. I could see Azzedine crying quietly in the corner. He couldn't understand why I had found such hope in what we had been told. I said to him, 'I've just found out I am carrying two little boys, and they are going to be absolutely beautiful. I have already picked out names for them that I know you are going to love!' Azzedine looked at me completely bewildered. I explained to him that I wanted to name the boys Hassan, meaning prince, and Hussein, meaning handsome prince. Some years previously I had watched a documentary with Azzedine on war-torn Afghanistan. I vividly recall one particular family, who had been living in dire poverty amid terrible atrocities. They had nothing between them and the elements but a ragged tent, and yet they seemed so completely happy because they had these precious little twin boys called Hassan and Hussein. Even though they had nothing, in my eyes they had everything.

Azzedine, however, was looking at our situation in a completely different light. To him, we were pregnant with conjoined babies— these two boys who were not going to live—and his heart was broken from the grief of it all, a grief from which he didn't believe he would ever recover. But I was having these boys, my sons. From that point on I began to make myself believe, day in and day out, that they were going to live against the odds. All I could think about was how I was going to do everything I could to bring that precious cargo safely into this world. One day I was going to see them happy and free, see them playing like other children, see them talk to one another, running wild with their sisters, swimming like little silvery fish in the sea. That's all I've ever wanted.

I had spent eight weeks grieving for these babies, who were to be lost to us, but then, on the joyous day I discovered they had two hearts, everything changed. From that day on I began to call these miraculous boys my 'Little Fighters'. Everyone around me had been so negative, so down about the complications—they believed this was just one long, living nightmare, which would ultimately end with their tiny lifeless bodies—whereas now I had wonderful hope shining through the chinks. The golden light of it dappled everything around me, and gave me strength to continue on that difficult journey. I went home that day and opened up the shutters in my home, threw open the windows and loosened the chains around my heart. I saw this as a chance, and thought: 'I am going to fight for these two.' I dared to let that elusive hope back into our homes, our lives and our hearts.

I awoke the following morning and decided to take my two girls to Dublin Zoo by train. Their whole summer had been shrouded in grief and darkness, and I wanted them to have at least one happy memory. Azzedine thought this a terrible idea. He was worried I would miscarry while I was on the train, but I was determined to give my children at least one day out. I said to him, 'These are my two Little Fighters, Azzedine, and they are not going to die!' I was convinced I was carrying two healthy boys who were going to live, going to defy everyone and everything. I could tell that Azzedine was worried that I was in denial, but I didn't care. I took the girls to the zoo that day. It was their first time on a train, and they were very excited, grinning and singing all the way. My aunt Marie and her children Stephen and Zachary, who live in Dublin, met us at the train station. Marie and I exchanged an emotional embrace; it was our first time meeting since I had told her about the twins eight weeks earlier. I remember our children running and playing and the warmth of their laughter felt like sunshine on my face. The joy of them being free, and running wild. It felt bizarre that in the space of 24 hours everything had changed, and I no longer felt like a ghost in my own life. Happiness began to run once again in my veins. From then on I decided to eat healthily and to get eight hours sleep a night. I threw off that awful dressing gown that had been my shroud and crawled out of my hollow shell. I was determined to get back to where I was before this hurricane hit our lives, smashing all that we held dear to pieces. I decided to phone Mr Kiely in London to tell him that the boys had two hearts, and asked him again for his opinion. This time he told me that was very positive news, and now, perhaps, CUMH could formally refer us to GOSH. It was the happy news I had been waiting to hear; it was hope.

As the weeks went on I began to really get to know my boys: Hassan, my quiet twin, was to my left, while Hussein, the boisterous one, was to my right. I could feel their distinct personalities even in the womb. Hussein was always fussing and moving on my right, while my happy Hassan was, as he is to this day, tranquil and sleepy. Little by little things got back to normal, but as the pregnancy became more visible it became harder to hide it from people. Each time somebody congratulated me, it felt like salt in a wound. I spent a lot of time just asking God over and over 'Why me?' What had I done wrong? I did everything I was supposed to do. We had planned this pregnancy carefully. What did I do that was so bad that I deserved this punishment? And that was exactly what it felt like, punishment. One day a very close friend and neighbour, Betty, whom I had told about the twins, arrived at my home to visit me. She was expecting a baby, but she was such a supportive friend and so mindful of my feelings that she found it hard to share her wonderful news with me. I could tell straight away she was struggling to tell me something. I eventually guessed what it was, and asked her if she was pregnant. We shed tears that day as I congratulated her; Betty had been nervous about telling me but I reassured her that I was fine, that I wanted her to enjoy her pregnancy. I begged her not to feel sad for me, because no matter what, I too was going to be a Mum regardless of how much time I was going to have with those precious babies.

One of the most painful things I had to learn to accept during this difficult time was just how lonely it could be and just how little support Azzedine and I had. As my scans continued, week in and week out, I would stay up into the early hours of the morning looking at pictures of other conjoined twins on the internet, wondering what my babies would look like, my eyes watering from the glare of the computer screen and the sting of my tears. Azzedine hated this; he did not want to see what I saw. He thought what I was doing was unhealthy, but I felt powerless. I wanted to know what we were facing. I knew no set of conjoined twins ever looked the same, so I would have to wait until the delivery to see what my little babies would look like, wait to see if they would ever breathe, or cry out for their Mummy. When I would ask Azzedine why he thought this had happened to us, and why we were being punished, he would say 'Whatever God gives to us, we have to accept.' I felt like shaking him when he said this. It angered me. I thought it a ridiculous concept, an impossible faith. We simply didn't deserve this; there was no justice or order to it. It was chaos. I didn't understand his way of thinking at all. Later, the very first time I held their precious bodies, I understood it perfectly.

————

During my second pregnancy, with Iman, I had discovered a website about 3D, ultrasound imaging. I remember being really excited when I read that the scan produced a live, 3D image of your baby in the womb and afterwards you could go home with some digital stills and a DVD to show your family. The scans, according to the website, could capture everything from a yawn to a stretch to the precious beating of the baby's heart inside the womb. It had been too late by the time I discovered this when I was pregnant with Iman, so when I found out I was pregnant again I phoned up a company called Baby Scan in Ballincollig to ask them at what stage I should come in. They told me that between 24 and 30 weeks was the best time for a clear image so I had been very much looking forward to booking one, but when at 12 weeks we were given our shattering news, obviously this took a back seat. I didn't really think about it again for a long time. In fact, the very thought of seeing these babies, whom I was sure I was going to lose, chilled me. But, after the 20-week scan, when I found out my boys each had a heart, I began to consider it as an option again. I really wanted to have a DVD and images of them when they were alive and kicking in my womb. I wanted something I could hold on to in case their precious lungs never breathed air. Some friends and family were very worried about my decision; they believed I could be setting myself up for more agony if the babies didn't make it. I think they had this image of me sitting at home, bereaved, watching the DVD obsessively and it terrified them. But after a lot of thought I decided that no matter what happened to these little guys, it would be a good thing to have a lasting image of them alive and moving. I couldn't see why this would be a negative thing, so I phoned the owner of the business, Paula Tunney, and asked for her discretion, as obviously I needed this to be carried out in the strictest confidence. She was extremely sensitive to our needs. She told me she would send a special sonographer down from Dublin to their centre in Ballincollig for the day, and reassured me that nobody would be told. I booked us in for a date in September and, despite all the trepidation, I looked forward to it with each passing day.

I remember feeling excited and nervous that day as I lay back on the bed in front of a large screen. With us I had brought along my Dad, my Aunt Val and my cousin's wife Sinead and there was a hushed silence in the room as everyone waited to see Hassan and Hussein. As the sonographer began to scan, I heard everyone gasp simultaneously, and there they were in 3D: our Little Fighters. Nothing prepared me for that moment. I couldn't believe I was seeing these babies as if I were in there floating with them. I became overwhelmed at the sight of their little bodies and burst into tears. Seeing a grainy image of a growing foetus on a hospital monitor is one thing, but this was like nothing I had ever imagined. I felt as if I could reach out and touch them. Seeing the faces of those little boys was too much to take; they were perfect, and beautiful, despite the fact that they were conjoined. I sobbed into Azzedine's arm as we watched them floating together, pushing backwards and forwards, their tiny arms around one another's shoulders; it was absolutely heart-breaking.

The girls were so excited. They squealed in delight as they picked out the little eyes, noses and mouths on the screen. Then, as the sonographer slowly moved the wand down across my lower belly, she suddenly shouted, 'Look everyone, look at their hands!' At that moment we saw what seemed like a miraculous event: the babies' two tiny hands had clasped together. I couldn't believe this. Here were two tiny babies, just 24 weeks in the womb, and you could see such a connection, such love between them. I looked around and everyone in the room was in tears. This powerful image was a picture of hope that carried me through the rest of that pregnancy. I felt grateful that at least the girls had seen their brothers alive and moving, even if they would never hold them, or smell them, or kiss them in this life.

Finally, the sonographer let us listen to their hearts beating, and as I listened to this happy thumping, I prayed for their lives. She printed off reams of photos for us that day in case that would be all that we would have left of our babies in the end. I just couldn't stop looking at the images of my boys. They were so handsome; even at this early stage I could see it. I held the miraculous little image of them in my mind always. I felt no matter what happened during the pregnancy, they had each other, and they would look after each other always. I told myself that even if they didn't make it, they would be together forever, bound together by love. The next day I purchased a large picture frame that had nine slots for photographs. I spent hours arranging and rearranging the little 3D images into those slots before placing it by my bed. I was so proud of those boys. I loved waking every morning to those wonderful images of hope.

Chapter 3 ∿

AN UNEXPECTED DEVELOPMENT

It was late October 2009 when we received word that we had to travel to the UK for a day of tests at both University College London Hospital (UCLH) and Great Ormond Street Hospital (GOSH). I was heavily pregnant when Azzedine and I, along with Marion Cunningham, the twins' sonographer, boarded an early flight for the UK from Cork Airport. As I half walked, half waddled up the creaking steps to the plane, I smiled as I looked forward to learning more about how my Little Fighters were faring. We eventually found our seats amid the polished businessmen, and sat down. I craned my neck to see the first light breaking through the dewy, oval-shaped window, Azzedine's hand in mine as the plane climbed into the clouds. I felt the boys move and kick with life inside me as the autumn sun came up over the horizon and produced a mesmerising funnel of light, which poured into the plane and warmed my face. I had never even considered the possibility that we could be in for more hardship that day, more impossibly difficult news. Had I known then what was to come, I don't think I would have ever mustered the strength to board that plane. The storm ahead would tear the fragile new buds of hope from my very soul, and cruelly trample on my nestling dreams.

When we reached UCLH, already tired from the journey, we were met by a very large group of doctors, nurses and midwives. Among them was an obstetrician, Mr Pat O'Brien, originally from Sunday's Well in Cork. I was delighted to meet a fellow Corkonian among this sea of strangers; it felt like a welcome and happy coincidence that the man who would bring my little boys into the world shared my hometown. His demeanour was calm and reassuring, yet authoritative; he immediately put me at ease. I learned that he had been a consultant at UCLH since 1999, and specialised in maternal medicine and high risk obstetrics, which is why he was the best choice when it came to delivering our boys.

When the first raft of tests and scans was completed, Azzedine and I were taken into a room by some members of the team to discuss the findings. We could not have anticipated what was to come. They told us we should prepare ourselves for the possibility that the boys had only two legs between them; they thought the other two had never formed. I simply couldn't believe this. I thought: 'How can this be happening to us? How can there be more pain for us, and for our boys? Have we not suffered enough?' I felt anger and pain rise up in my throat at this dreadful news; I thought I was going to be sick. The medics in Cork had always believed that the boys had two arms and two legs each, and now here we were being dealt another crushing blow, and at this late stage. The doctors told me I would have to undergo an MRI scan later that day at GOSH to confirm the test results, so within a matter of hours we were transported to that hospital with this terrible news between us like an unwelcome stranger. Because I was so heavily pregnant, I had to be helped into the MRI machine. It was deafeningly loud inside; I was so terrified that my heart thumped in my chest. I felt the babies become more and more distressed inside me and I stroked my belly to try to calm them, tears streaming down my face. Looking back now I realise I was in a complete state of shock that day. I just went into autopilot as the doctors carried out what seemed like an endless series of tests, while that new knowledge was slowly dripping into my mind, like a slow-release poison. I no longer wanted to hear anything they were going to tell me; I longed to just curl up in my own bed.

When the tests were finally completed we were sent away to allow the doctors at both hospitals to review and compare results. I will never forget that endless hour sitting in a cafe, staring out the window onto an autumnal London scene, fallen leaves dancing in the wind as hundreds of busy Londoners flew by, busy in their lives while mine was slowly being picked apart, piece by painful piece. I couldn't eat anything; I felt nauseous and frightened. The fear of it thumped in my ears. I realise now I had started out on that journey far too full of hope, far too full of positivity. I had been deluded when I thought they were going to discover all of these wonderful things and tell me my babies were thriving. Now, looking back, I know you should never allow yourself to be too positive amid such murky uncertainty, the truth hanging like the sword of Damocles above your head, ready to strike at any moment. I foolishly almost had a skip in my step boarding the plane in Cork that morning. I had been convinced that things had turned around for us; little did we know that the worst was yet to come.

After that endless black hour we began to walk back to the hospital in silence to meet the surgeons. Mr Kiely and his colleague, Prof Agostino Pierro, were waiting for us in one of the consultant's rooms. It was my first time meeting Mr Kiely in person, after speaking to him a number of times on the phone. Through his veneer of professionalism I could immediately tell from his expression that he had something grave to tell me. He quietly explained to us that our boys shared the pericardium sac that surrounds and protects the heart, that one of the twins had a hole in his heart, and they had only one leg each; the other legs hadn't formed at all. He also told us they were joined from chest to pelvis and shared a gut, a bladder and a liver. I just remember wondering what this awful piercing sound was before realising it was coming from me. It was absolutely horrific. It felt like the first time I was told the babies were conjoined all over again. I had believed in my heart we were going to get good news during that trip, that we were going to go home with renewed hope. I really thought this new revelation would push me over the precipice to which I had been edging ever closer for months. It was bad enough that the twins were joined and shared organs, but now they were missing limbs too! I felt angry at the world, abandoned by it.

Impossibly there was even more to come. Mr Kiely went on to tell us that if the boys were deemed unsuitable for separation, they would spend their lives together, unable to stand, unable to walk, with no quality of life. He also told me their lifespan could be shortened considerably if they were not separated because their hearts shared the pericardium sac. I began to struggle to see and breathe amid the blinding aftershock of this cluster bomb that had crashed down on our lives. I glimpsed those tiny babies in my mind, bound together for an eternity, and the pain of it stabbed at me relentlessly. I imagined them half-grown, endlessly couch bound, endlessly staring out of a window at children at play, endlessly lonely for life.

I realised I had been gripping the side of the chair so tightly that my hands had begun to ache. Azzedine prised my hand off the chair and told me we were going to have to leave the hospital and make our way back to Heathrow. I dreaded walking out of the hospital with that new knowledge bearing down on us, chasing us down the runway, on to the plane. I knew we had to leave if we were going to catch our flight home, but my legs just refused to cooperate. They felt like heavy jelly as we walked out of the room. I headed straight for the nearest bathroom, locked the door and just wailed for my unborn children. I could hear Azzedine knocking, trying to get in, but I just couldn't get up off the floor. Our sonographer Marion also tried to help and comfort me but I was lost and heartbroken. Eventually Azzedine coaxed me out, and I managed to get myself together.

We slowly set off on the 10-minute walk from the hospital to the nearest tube station, but this time it felt like a thousand miles; Azzedine half carried me there. It was rush hour in London, so the tube was heaving with rows of tightly packed bodies. There I was in a corner, heavily pregnant, sobbing uncontrollably, trying to hide my face as best I could. The other passengers were either staring at me or, more obviously, trying not to. When I got off at Heathrow I could barely walk. The airport personnel had to get me a wheelchair, and I was pushed from the terminal right up to the gate. I remembered I had promised the girls a present from London, so I sent Azzedine back to the Duty Free to get them something. It was heartbreaking to see him walk back: a broken man laden down with bags of chocolates and teddies. We both just cried and held on to one another as we waited for the boarding call. I held on to Azzedine for dear life all the way home, still sobbing uncontrollably as the flight assistants looked on helplessly. I stared at the picture of my happy, heart-shaped boys that I carried around in my wallet, and mourned for them all over again.

When the plane finally touched down, and we got back to our home in Carrigtwohill, it was long past midnight. Azzedine and I stole into the girls' room, and gently took them from their beds and cradled their sleeping bodies in our arms. The comfort of their smooth little backs felt like home. We needed them at that moment, more than ever. My Aunt Val looked on helplessly as we just cried and cried.

Waking the next day with that knowledge was unspeakably difficult. I couldn't discuss with anyone what we had been told. I was back in that dark, terrifying and empty place, and this time I thought I would never crawl out. I couldn't accept there was still more heartache in store for us, and more pain in store for the twins. They were already sharing a liver, the gut, and the bladder and now they were missing limbs too. I couldn't handle any more. I didn't want to tell anyone about it, because I felt if I talked about it, it would become real. As much as I tried not to think about it, the spectre of it hung over everything like a menacing gloom. I put away my framed pictures of their scans; I could no longer bear to look at them—they no longer represented hope but an unstoppable freight train of pain. All my family knew was that something horrendous had been revealed to us in London, a terrible thing I could not find the strength to discuss. Weeks went by before I finally told my father and my Aunt Val what we had been told. The hardest part to accept was the knowledge that I could do nothing to change any of it. The boys had only two legs; they might never walk, that's if they lived at all. As a mother you want to fix things for your babies, and I knew I couldn't fix this. Every throb of their hearts on that monitor broke mine over and over and over again. Facing the loss of one child is hard, but two is impossible.

Within days it was time for us to return for our weekly scans at CUMH. Ever since the medics in London had discovered the boys were missing limbs, I noticed a change in my husband. He could no longer face going back to the hospital in Cork and sitting through those scans. I could tell he was trying to be strong for me, but it was tearing him apart to see those little boys grow, knowing that pretty much everything was stacked against them. The fact that the twins were facing such a massive disadvantage, even if they did survive, murdered our hopes. I had to go into that miserable room a number of times without my husband or with my Dad, my Aunt Val, or the girls, faking smiles through my agony. I hated going without Azzedine but I knew he needed relief from the onslaught that was slowly breaking his spirit. Eventually I convinced him to come back for me. He agreed, but I knew he just sat there silently for my benefit; he had clearly given up. He didn't ask questions any more; he didn't want to look at the screen any more. I lost him for a while.

———

November's dank chill began to set in, and eventually the doctors in London and Cork began to piece together a plan for the birth. The boys' original due date had been 10 January, which is also my birthday, but now they were to be delivered six weeks prematurely, at UCLH on 2 December. The staff at CUMH tried to convince me that Azzedine and I should travel to London on 30 November alone, that we should leave the girls in Cork. They believed the experience would be much more difficult for us with the girls in tow, but we knew Malika and Iman gave us strength. We also knew that if they were with us, we would have to keep going for them. Realistically we didn't know how long we would be in London—it could have been a matter of days if the boys didn't survive, or months if they did. We decided as a family that whatever time, if any, those little guys were going to have, we were all going to be there to share it. We had gone through everything as a family, from that first scan, which shattered our world, to this moment. The girls had grown to love their brothers. They were always kissing and stroking my bump. Iman would suddenly yank up my jumper and stroke my belly with her little angelic hands, and say, 'Mummy, I love my brothers', gazing up at me with her gorgeous brown eyes. We knew we were going to have to finish this journey as a family no matter what lay ahead.

My amazingly supportive Aunt Val offered to come out to London for a few weeks with us for the birth, so we knew it was going to be possible to be all together. I don't believe I would have made it through my pregnancy if it was not for my two girls. It was during that bleak summer that Michael Jackson died, and his most popular songs were playing on a loop on the radio. Malika was forever singing his song 'You Are Not Alone' as she decided that this was the boys' song. She and little Iman would often sing it to their twin brothers who lived in Mummy's tummy. I vividly remember them sitting on the end of my bed, with their little arms around one other, singing slightly out of tune and at the top of their voices. Later, when the babies were lying in the Neonatal Intensive Care Unit in London, I saw with amazement on the small plasma screen TV above their cot that this very song had been taken up by the 'X Factor' contestants as a charity Christmas single, with all the proceeds going to GOSH where my children were being cared for.

———

A couple of weeks before the birth I had decided to approach the then Minister for Foreign Affairs, Micheál Martin, to ask him for his help. It was early November when Azzedine and I, heavily pregnant, walked into his clinic to share our big secret. I noticed a look of recognition flash across his face when he saw me, as we had met before. I first met with him in January 2009, after spending most of that preceding Christmas being horrified by news footage of the Israeli invasion of the Gaza Strip on 27 December 2008. Over the course of three days we had seen relentless images of children dying and suffering, and it really affected me. I couldn't bear to watch the torture and murder of innocents without doing something to help. I decided to ask a number of local pharmacists in east Cork if they could spare some medical supplies for the children of Gaza. They were all more than happy to help. I then went to the Midleton Park Hotel to ask if they would have any spare blankets. They gave me more than 600. A number of other hotels also contributed, so finally we put everything we had collected in a huge container to be sent off to Gaza. The day the container was set to be shipped out, Minister Martin came down, and we had our photograph taken with him. He was lovely in person, and I thought he was someone I could talk to easily.

Looking back now to January 2009, it is strange to think my biggest fear and source of anguish were these poor children of

Gaza and their suffering. I would never have imagined that a few months later I would be worrying for the lives of my own precious boys. I remember Azzedine telling me how, according to the Muslim faith, if you do something kind for someone, their prayers will come back to help you in your hour of need. He said to me, 'Every blanket you sent to Gaza that warmed somebody's child, their prayers will come back to help you; every medicine you sent that healed someone, their prayers will come back to help you too.' I was amazed at how this belief later comforted me in my time of need. So when we walked into Minister Martin's clinic I presume he must have assumed we had returned to discuss the Gaza issue, but as we sat down and told him of our situation he dropped his pen and just listened to us, sympathy etched across his face. From that day on, he made sure we had at least some level of support every step of the way. For this, I will always be grateful. I fought back tears as I explained to him that we didn't know what to do if our babies died while we were in London. He was extremely reassuring and kind. He promised us he would do his best to help. For us, the worst case scenario would mean we would be stuck in London with our two daughters trying to make arrangements to bring two dead babies home for burial.

The fact that we had to travel to London for the birth, away from our home, our friends and our neighbours, really frightened me. Nobody could ever guarantee me that the boys would live, and I dreaded being stuck over in London if the worst happened. I did not know who would be able to help me if the babies didn't make it. I couldn't handle the feeling of helplessness and uncertainty any more, so one afternoon, without telling anyone, I decided to phone a local funeral home to ask about a plot for my boys. This is one of the hardest things I have ever done, or am ever likely to do. The receiver shook violently in my hand as I asked the funeral director what we should do if our worst fears were confirmed and we had to bring two tiny babies home to be buried. She reassured me that GOSH would be able to help us with the arrangements, so I hung up the phone and broke down. I had pleaded with the medics in Cork to allow me to have my babies in Cork, but they told me I couldn't as they just didn't have the expertise when it came to conjoined twins; the risk would be far too high. The looming prospect of having to leave for London on 30 November for the birth truly terrified me. I was afraid to go over there pregnant and whole, and return home empty and hollow.

Nevertheless we soon had to think about what to pack to bring with us to London. I felt really upset when I asked at the hospital what I should bring for the babies, and was told I should bring only a minimal number of things. Usually, as all Mums know, when you go into hospital to have a baby you are told to bring three babygrows, vests and nappies, a variety of little things for your newborn. I remembered happily and excitedly packing my bags when I was due to give birth to Malika and Iman, folding the impossibly small babygrows that would soon be filled out with a perfect little body, but now my bag seemed as empty as my soul. One afternoon, however, I received a call from a midwife at UCLH, Mae Nugent. She said in her broad Co. Armagh accent, 'I am just calling to give you a list of things you will need for the babies.' It lifted my spirits when she told me I should pack two little hats and two little booties. She told me the hospital had the same policy for all Mums, whether their babies lived for 10 days, 10 minutes or 10 precious seconds. She told me not to bring babygrows, but to bring a baby blanket, and that my girls should buy the boys two little teddy bears to put in their cot. She also told me that parents are always encouraged to bring a family photograph that would be placed on the babies' cot; basically it seemed the policy was to surround the babies with love from the moment they were born, and this filled me with hope. This woman's words meant so much to me at a time when I felt lonely, desperate and low. She remained a constant support to me throughout my time at UCLH, and continues to be a support even now. She truly is one of the most amazingly selfless people I have ever met; sometimes she seemed like an angel to us in our black despair.

Packing up for London was extremely difficult, as there was so much uncertainty involved. We had been told if the twins did survive they could be in GOSH for several months, or we could be home in a matter of days if they died. Very few people knew that we were having conjoined twins, and here we were about to just disappear from our locality like thieves in the night. All anybody knew was that there were complications with my pregnancy, and the loneliness of that secret was like an icy winter in my heart.

Eventually we finished packing and prepared to head into the unknown. I was so heavily pregnant at this stage that I could barely manoeuvre myself into the car. Closing up the house was very difficult. It was hard to put the key into that door and lock up our lives and our hearts, not knowing whether the next time the key slinked back in the lock we would have our two sons with us. I felt that our lives had been frozen behind that door until we returned to free them. My cousin Brendan collected us and took us to the airport and I remember how difficult it was for him to say goodbye.

My father found it extremely hard to see us go; the last time I saw him before we left for London he practically ran from the house. I think he was frightened that he would lose me. He was frightened for all of us, and for what we faced. He wanted to hide that fear from me lest it drag me down further into that dank, dark hole. He feared for my life as I feared for my boys. He couldn't talk to his friends and neighbours about it as I had sworn him to secrecy, and I know those close to him were confused by the sudden change in him. The secrecy was killing me too. In those last few days before we stole away and boarded yet another flight I would find myself talking to a neighbour and just wanting to blurt it all out, to lance that swollen, heavy secret. The isolation of it was horrendous, but we knew we had to keep it quiet. Azzedine and I were hanging in there by a gradually fraying thread; we were just not strong enough to let people into our private nightmare. We knew we had to do this alone, see it through to the bitter end as a family.

Chapter 4 ✣

‖ LONDON

It was a cold and dreary November morning in the dark heart of winter when once again we boarded a plane for London. At 34 weeks pregnant, I felt absolutely enormous as I climbed the steps to the aircraft; in one hand I clutched a letter from the hospital that permitted me to fly, while I held Iman with the other. I tried to hide my despair, but my ghostly pallor and red-rimmed eyes gave it all away. There must have been more than 250 people on the flight, and as I struggled to waddle down the central aisle, one by one this sea of faces turned towards me. I wanted desperately to get to our seats as a red heat began to creep from my neck up to my cheeks. I noticed one man looking at my bump with his mouth wide open, which made me very uneasy. We were trying to laugh and joke a little for the girls' sake, but I would have done anything not to have been on that wretched plane, getting ever closer to inevitable pain.

When we eventually got to our seats, I realised with embarrassment that the seatbelt just wouldn't fit around my bump, so I had to call the air hostess to fetch me another one to stretch it out—and, as Iman insisted on sitting on my lap, another seatbelt had to be added on. I remember Azzedine and Val giggled about this, which broke the stifling tension a little. There were light-hearted moments peppered here and there on that journey, but I think these were mostly precipitated by stress. We were all so haunted by worry that it was a case of either laughing or going mad. But, in the quieter moments, as the plane cut through the clouds, my mind began to wander to a darker place. The terrifying thought that within the next 48 hours my babies would either be born or lost haunted me. I imagined how I would feel if some day all of us were boarding a plane home, all six of us, together, happy and laughing in the sunlight. A sharp kick from my Little Fighters shook me out of my daydreaming and back to reality. As the plane cut through the clouds, I begged God with all my heart to let my beloved twins survive. At that moment I knew I would have readily swapped my life for theirs. All too soon the pilot announced our descent into London. I held on to my little girl as my baby boys kicked with life inside me.

––––––

It had taken a lot of convincing to get Malika to go to London. The week before we left she told me she didn't want to leave her friends or her home. She kept saying to me, 'Mummy, I don't want to go to the other world!' and at first I didn't know what to tell her. She was a big fan of 'The X Factor' at the time, and I explained to her how London was 'X Factor' land, where Simon Cowell lived. She was so excited at hearing this that she raced up the stairs to pack her things, including her gold 'Alexandra' dress. The poor thing was set to explode from delight as she pulled her pink suitcase down the stairs behind her shouting, 'Mummy, Mummy, I'm going to meet Simon Cowell!', the case thumping off every step. Later, when we were at the boys' side, I remember wishing that the 'X Factor' judges would come in to visit the sick children, so she wouldn't be disappointed, but by then she was excited by her brothers and forgot all about it.

My poor brown-eyed girl had found it hard to leave her school, and her friends. She was as bright as a button: a model student. She loved her class teacher, Miss Tuttle, and was very upset at the thought of leaving all her friends behind, especially for an indefinite period of time—even a month to a child can seem like a lifetime. Other Mums at the school had told me their little ones were upset by the fact that Malika was going off to London, as they did not fully understand why. There was an emotional goodbye with the few Mums who knew of my situation on that last rainy day of school. We didn't know if the next time we met I would have either of my beloved twins. I decided to let Malika hold a party with her classmates and it broke my heart to think I was taking her away from her life. I had told her school principal, Mrs Moran, and her teacher about the twins so they would have a full understanding of our situation. I wanted them to keep a close eye on my little girl, in case she ever felt saddened or overwhelmed by our situation. Malika also had to say goodbye to her friends and teacher at her swimming class, which she had attended every Saturday for the previous two years. I loved watching her swim like a little tawny otter in the pool, waving to me with her big, bright smile. She was devastated that she had to leave it all behind her and I felt down that Malika was upset. It was such a hard time for her, and yet she handled the whole situation better than any adult. I really saw my little girl grow up overnight. She was wonderful; she gave me such strength.

The pregnancy had been such a lonely time, almost like a death. Nobody understood what I was going through; all I really had were my girls to keep me sane. You go to a hospital, week after endless week, for scans and tests and more scans and yet the doctors can't give you the answers you need because they just don't have them. It was frustrating. I felt the doctors should know everything, but because conjoined twins are so rare, nobody understood how I felt, so I turned to the internet and documentaries for information. Malika would often come in and out of the room while I was watching some medical documentary, but I assumed she barely noticed. However, about one month before the birth, she came to my bedroom one Saturday evening and sat on the edge of my bed. I knew by the way she was shuffling and looking at me that there was something on her mind, so I sat down and asked her if everything was OK. She looked at me intently and asked, 'Mummy, are our babies stuck together?' I was speechless; the fact that my five-year-old girl had asked this question astounded me. I knew she didn't understand the word 'conjoined', and yet there she was asking me whether our babies were joined together. I thought for a second before answering. I didn't want to lie to her; these were her little brothers, and I felt she had a right to know. I held her chin in my hand and looked right at her and said, 'Yes, Malika, your brothers are stuck together.' She looked at me, her big brown eyes darkening, and asked, 'But why would God do that to them?' I could see there were tears forming in her eyes so, thinking on my feet, I replied, 'Do you know the way every night you come in to my room for cuddles?' She nodded. 'Well, when the boys were in my tummy they were cuddling and kissing each other so much that they got stuck together, the silly beggars!' At this, she laughed a hearty child's laugh and said, 'They are my silly little brothers!' As she left the room, I called after her. She turned and smiled, and I knew she was happy with the explanation. I felt relieved. I could tell this had been troubling her for quite a while. As soon as she got her answer, she felt better and she stopped worrying; she moved on from it. Instead of fearing it now she thought of it as a funny and happy thing. In the weeks that followed she would often ask me, 'Mummy, are my brothers still stuck together?' It became this humorous thing between us. She and Iman gave up a great deal over that year, and they never got upset or angry; they just continued to love and kiss this growing little bundle inside my tummy. They willed the boys to live. I think my Little Fighters knew how much they were loved before they were even born.

——

We touched down in Heathrow with a bump and were met off the plane by one of the airport personnel, who had been sent to bring me a wheelchair. I remember I was so heavy that he had great difficulty pushing me up the ramp. He had quite a slight build, and I could tell he was really struggling. I could hear Azzedine and Val in fits of laughter a little behind me; it felt good to release the pressure with these moments of comedy that suddenly erupted somewhere between our fear and hysteria. It got even more comical when we eventually made our way down to the baggage collection area and I got to watch Azzedine falling over the four big suitcases, all the babies' things, the girls' bags and Iman's buggy. I sat in my wheelchair and laughed as Azzedine performed what seemed like a comedy act, trying to get all our things off the carousel. It felt strange to be laughing at the time, but again it was either laugh or cry, and my children had seen enough tears to drown all of us. We decided to drop the bags off at a pokey flat we had rented, as it was near the hospital. It was such an awful, Dickensian place: grimy and dank, with about eight flights of stairs leading up to it. Poor Azzedine had to act the donkey again and drag all the cases up the endless stairwell; I was incapable of helping him because I was so heavily pregnant. I hated the thought of my little girls being stuck in that wretched place, but for now we didn't have a choice. We decided to take them to a McDonald's before going to the hospital, as we knew it would be a while before we would do something again as a family.

All the laughter and the light-heartedness that was getting us through that ominous day vanished when we arrived at UCLH. It loomed above us: a terrifying vista of what might or might not be. I told the receptionist who I was, but neither she, nor anybody else, seemed to have any idea what I was doing there. I found this all very strange and unsettling, as I had received calls from the staff just minutes before we arrived to check whether we were near the hospital. After some confusion, we were met by a member of the boys' team who explained to us that, in fact, as a security precaution, very few staff at that sprawling hospital had been told about us. It felt bizarre: here we were, this ordinary family from Cork, and yet all the people around us were talking about security and secrecy, and doing everything to keep our presence there from becoming public knowledge.

We were shown to a private room and were just settling in when there was a rap on the door. A kindly man, named Tony McCullagh, from the Irish embassy walked in. He had been sent to visit me by Minister Micheál Martin. I could tell from his face that he felt genuinely sad for us, and did not really know what to say. He became a wonderful support to us in London, and it was good to know that somebody, among those millions of Londoners, was looking out for us, watching over us in our time of need. He was quite an avuncular character, and he played and laughed with Malika and Iman and brought an air of normality to an afternoon that felt heavy and claustrophobic.

After an hour or so he said goodbye, and left Azzedine, the girls, and I alone in that lonely room. We chatted nervously to pass the time, trying to avoid thinking of what lay ahead of us amid the hospital smell and the fear. I could see the wan and sickly winter sun had dropped through my grey hospital window, and the dark begin to settle in. I knew Azzedine and the girls would have to leave soon, leave me with that monstrous fear that I could feel biding its time until I was alone. I didn't want to be by myself in that purgatory from which I could hear the soft cries of babies and the chatter of their blissfully happy mothers. With a heavy heart I wondered whether I would ever get to hear my babies cry.

It was unsettling to feel my little ones move inside me, and to know that these could be their last days. In a way, it seemed it would be better if they stayed where they were, inside me. I wondered how my two little boys would look when they came out. I had seen their beautiful faces on the 3D scans, and no matter what they shared, I knew they were my special little boys. They meant more to me than life itself. All that was certain was that they were joined from chest to pelvis, shared the pericardium sac that surrounded their hearts, and that they also shared a liver, a gut and a bladder. Obviously we had been told they had one leg each, but as the doctors said, they could not be certain of anything until the boys were born and were in front of our very eyes. I secretly wished that they had got it wrong about the boys' legs. I imagined the moment of their birth and how it would feel if I saw that they actually had two legs each. I convinced myself there was so much kicking going on from all angles in my tummy, that maybe, just maybe, they had been wrong about it.

All too soon I had to say goodbye to my family. The moment the door closed my mind started to race and race through what lay ahead; almost every eventuality filled me with dread. I did not fear for my own life—if it was a choice between my children or me, I would always choose them. For me, a mother always chooses her babies—it was the thought of having to go on if I lost them that haunted me. I didn't sleep a wink that night. The sharp buzz of patients ringing the nurses' bells kept waking me with a start every time I began to doze off. The general clatter of the hospital ward did little to soothe my mind. The nursing staff at UCLH were an incredibly caring bunch. They literally spent the whole night going in and out of patients' rooms making sure they had everything they could possibly need. They went way beyond the call of duty when it came to my care too. They gave me a true understanding of why people sometimes refer to the nursing profession as a vocation.

The following morning, my midwife Mae Nugent came to see me, a welcome face amid the murky misery. She never failed to lift my spirits. Indeed, in my bleaker moments, when all I could do was despair, she used to tell me that anything was possible, and now I know she was right. Our clinical psychotherapist at UCLH, Kati Grey, also came to see me that morning to offer her support. We talked through every eventuality in order to prepare me for the worst. She was a wonderfully supportive woman; she would often come to see me on her days off, laden down with gifts for me and the girls to cheer us. She reminded me of how many good people there were in the world. I had lost sight of that during my lonely pregnancy. I found myself surrounded by many strangers in London who were kind to me; some of them went on to become permanent friends, full of support and love.

After breakfast, Mae brought me down to meet the team, and to see where the surgery would take place. I was introduced to a very large group of medics who were going to perform the delivery. I felt incredibly nervous. I was trying to be pleasant, but I could not stop crying as I shook hand after hand. I was introduced to a nurse from Cork, Mary Dinan, and it was lovely to hear such a familiar accent in the middle of this sea of scrubs. I could barely walk at this stage I was so heavily pregnant. I remember being terrified as I was shown where I would be lying for the surgery: beneath an ominously large clock that I knew was already counting down the minutes.

I was also shown into an adjoining room where the boys were to be suctioned and ventilated after they came out. They would then be rushed off to GOSH. I had been told there was a big fear that their heads would be too close together to facilitate the ventilation tubes; this was a very frightening thing to hear. To my left, I saw all of these machines and equipment that were affixed with blue labels for Hassan, and green labels for Hussein. Everything was clearly divided for both twins. I was told all of the medical staff looking after Hassan would be wearing blue scrubs, and all of Hussein's team would be wearing green. There were at least 20 medical personnel involved in the procedure. There were Operation Department practitioners, Mr Pat O'Brien and two other obstetricians. There were scrub nurses, who handled the instruments, and runners, who run about getting things that are needed during the birth. There were two teams of paediatricians for the babies: one for Hassan, the other for Hussein. It did feel reassuring to see how prepared they were. It eased my mind a little to think they had done it all before, and that they were getting together later that day to run through the whole process step by step to make sure they were all clear about what exactly was going to happen. They told me that they were very hopeful for my boys, but I knew the statistics—they had been running amok in my mind for months, taunting me.

When we left to go back to my room, I noticed that a big screen and a barricade had been placed around the entrance to the theatre. I was told this was for security purposes, which again felt so strange. Here I was, this normal woman from Cork, with a normal husband and a normal life. I thought to myself: 'How did we get to this?' Only the people who were immediately involved in the birth in the hospital knew about the twins. I am still in awe to this day that it never got out.

Later that day, I had another scan and it transpired the boys had turned around inside me from the head down position to an upright state. They were now perched under my chest. Mr O'Brien told me not to worry about this, that it would all be OK. It was lovely to have a Cork connection with him. He had the most calm, reassuring voice I have ever heard, or am ever likely to hear. I think the staff at that hospital saw how much I longed for those babies, and how I didn't care what way they came out; I just wanted them so badly, and I know they wanted us to have our happy ending.

As the day ran into evening, I began to feel completely drained and exhausted. I could barely talk during those final tearful telephone conversations with the few people at home who knew. The girls and Azzedine came in to see me with Val for the last time, and we decided to make a little home movie of all of us together, in case it was the last time we were all together. The girls squealed with delight at my 'moving bump', and I smiled and laughed along, forcing the fear back down my throat until they left. It was a wonderful, family moment. Malika and Iman had always loved when they could see and feel the boys moving around inside my tummy, but all the laughter and their baby-teeth smiles was mixed with pain. I knew this could be the last time they got to feel their tiny brothers move, and this brought on a black and crushing sadness. I wanted it to be a special moment for them, and for us, but it was hard to hold back my tears. Malika handed me a lovely picture she had drawn for the twins, which depicted herself, her Mummy and Daddy, Iman and her two handsome little brothers, who always held hands. This picture was later taped to the boys' cot after their birth. It was Malika's picture of hope, her dream for all of us: together forever, her happy family. My children: so innocent, so happy. How were we going to tell them if the boys didn't make it? How were we supposed to take that happiness and crush it? I looked down on their two little heads and it took every last bit of strength not to bundle them up in my arms and run out of that hospital.

Finally, the moment I had been dreading was upon me: time to say goodbye. It was such a wrench. I had rarely been without my girls; they were upset, and I was upset. It was as if a knife were cutting through the fleshy bond between us and I could feel its every ridge. My Aunt Val's face was etched with pain and worry as she took the girls away to give Azzedine and myself some time alone. I squeezed their little bodies tight, sobbing silently into their hair, while Azzedine whispered to me to be strong, that we would get through this together. I was absolutely distraught saying goodbye to him as he begged me to try to get some sleep. I knew there was no chance I could close my eyes against that howling fear. I was practically vibrating with terror; I could feel each moment's passing, hurtling me closer and closer to that cold theatre table. I remember the worry on my husband's face as he left the room. I tried to fake a smile. I just wanted to go with him.

I wanted to call out after him to get me out of there, and to not make these poor little babies come into a world they might be too fragile to survive. That was one of the longest nights of my life. I lay alone hour after hour, minute after minute, in the eye of a storm that was raging in my mind, the haunting cry of babies never ceasing until dawn's light crept through my window.

The next morning Azzedine arrived looking pale and weary to find me sitting up in bed. I was utterly exhausted. I had wanted to sleep so badly, but just hadn't been able to. He looked very frightened, and I could tell he was trying to put on a front for me. From the moment the nurses and doctors came in to talk me through what was going to happen, I began to shake. It started off as a slight tremor in my hands, which soon saw my whole body shaking and vibrating uncontrollably. My teeth chattered in my head like a child's Halloween toy. I had no control over it. I had never felt fear like that before, the sheer violence of it. Mae Nugent, my midwife, came into the room to see me. The sight of her face was like being wrapped in a warm, comfortable blanket. She asked me to show her how to use our video camera so she could film parts of the birth, and take the first pictures of our boys when they came out. I collected up their two little hats, which had tiny prince motifs sewn onto them to represent the meaning of their names, and the two little teddies the girls had brought for them, and gave them to Mae.

Soon it was time to walk down that corridor, down towards my blackest fear. Azzedine held my hand as I cried uncontrollably; Mae, holding my other hand, tried to give me strength. Since last July we had had to cope with the fact that our boys were joined, and might not survive their first precious day, but now that the moment of truth was finally here, I realised with dread that we weren't ready at all. We had grown to love them dearly, they were so much a part of me, and I was frightened of losing them. I didn't want to put those terrifying statistics to the test. I remember the hushed silence and the sound of my husband's grief as we neared the theatre with its barriers and screens. I tried to make him laugh by saying I felt like I was walking The Green Mile, thinking I could joke through the tears for his sake, but there was no laughing this off. As the door to the theatre neared, my heart began to jump in my chest. I took a deep breath and thought: 'This is it.'

Chapter 5 ∿

| THE BIRTH

M y teeth were still chattering violently in my head as the theatre door swung shut behind me, an army of scrubs before me: blue for Hassan and green for Hussein. My breathing became more and more rapid as the giant clock ticked loudly on the wall. When Azzedine followed me in wearing scrubs, I barely recognised him. I was told the first step would involve an anaesthetic, and an epidural. The epidural was excruciating. The needle just would not hit home: it went in and out, and out and in, this hot jabbing that sent shockwaves of pain through my body. It was absolute agony. I kept grabbing Azzedine's arm and squeezing it, begging him to make it stop. I wanted to bellow at the top of my voice as a slick of cold sweat broke out all over my body. Eventually it did go in, but the jabbing had completely unsettled me. Each member of the team came and introduced themselves to me once again, and shook my hand. I could see how concerned they all were for what I was facing, perhaps for the responsibility they faced themselves. As frightened as I was for the lives of those babies, I knew I was surrounded by a highly functioning team who had gone through this procedure step by step; every detail, every eventuality—they had prepared for it. I had to just repeat to myself over and over again: 'They have done this before; they can get us through this!'

I remember Mr O'Brien talking me through what would happen, but all the time he was speaking to me my body kept shaking. I was etherised on the theatre table, pumped with high doses of morphine and painkillers to numb me from the chest down. The doctors then sprayed an ice-cold spritz on my body to see what I could feel, and eventually I couldn't feel anything. A blue screen was pulled in front of me to block my view of what was going on, but to my left I could still see the sharp, surgical instruments glinting in the cold, unforgiving light; the sight of them terrified me. Through all the nervousness I also felt very uncomfortable about my nudity, as there were more than 20 people in the room.

Then it started: that awful cutting below my breast bone. Because the boys had to be lifted out together at the same time, a normal, straight across, bikini-line Caesarean was not possible; the opening had to be much wider in depth. I had to have what is described as a Classical Caesarean, which runs in a vertical line along the length of my stomach. I was aware of the cutting, not in a painful way, but I recall being sickened by the cold, unearthly feel of it. My body shook so much that I felt as if I were practically levitating with fear. Mr O'Brien was telling me how he had cut through the first layer, and was about to cut open my stomach and then would go on to the next section, through to the womb. He had to pull my skin apart, and I could feel my insides being stretched. I was nauseated, aware of the pulling, pushing and tugging, feeling like I was being ripped apart. I held on to Azzedine, willing it to end.

After just a few minutes Mr O'Brien said he could see my boys. He told me to get ready, that he and the obstetricians were preparing to take the babies out. It took three of them to pull the boys out. They had to lift them together very carefully, as it would have been dangerous to stretch or place any pressure on the boys' join. I took a deep breath and braced myself. I felt this unbelievable tugging and pulling, which became almost unbearable as the three obstetricians lifted the boys together, and then, that golden cry, that delicious sound of life. I was relieved to hear it: it meant they were alive and breathing air, at least for now.

After the initial relief passed I started to panic. I was straining to see what was going on, and desperately asking if they were OK. I remember Mr O'Brien saying, 'OK, show Mum the babies,' and then I got my first, two-second glimpse of the beautiful duo from across the room, a bloodied towel around them, so fast, so fleeting—my boys. They came out holding one another in that sweet embrace. I was told they weighed just 9 lb, or 4.4 kg combined, so small, so precious. I burst into tears at the little happy-heart shape of them. A giant wave of emotion broke over me, almost drowning me with its force. I felt happy they were alive, but sad that they had complications. I was relieved the birth was over, but worried they wouldn't survive.

The doctors gently placed them on a special platform, and immediately rushed them into the adjoining room so the two teams of paediatricians could suction and ventilate them. I almost felt those awful tubes going down their throats, choking me too. I pleaded with Azzedine to leave my side, and check if they really did have only two legs. When he came back into the room, his face was wet with tears, so I knew. I found out later that after the medical staff had cleaned up the boys, they let their Daddy have a precious moment with them. Mae Nugent, our midwife, photographed it, and I cherish that beautiful image of Azzedine praying over our tiny babies to this day, his hands almost bigger than them. There was a hushed silence in the room as the staff waited for him to pray, these impossibly tiny hands holding his. I desperately wanted to see them with my own eyes. I wanted to count their fingers and toes, check what they did or didn't have, but I couldn't move.

It was then time to close me up, something I will never forget. Nothing could have prepared me for that unendurable and racking pain. I was scared, exhausted and traumatised before it even began. Mr O'Brien explained to me how my stomach would have to be stitched up first before the stapling could begin. The pain was hellish. I felt each and every one of those 70 staples like tiny, piercing knives puncturing my flesh, the white, blinding pain of them. I was begging Mr O'Brien to stop before he was even one-quarter of the way through. I just kept asking him over and over again how much longer it would take, and were my boys OK, crying uncontrollably all the time. The whole process took about 45 minutes; it seemed endless. Afterwards, I felt like Dr Frankenstein's monster, pieced together by scraps of stapled and stitched skin.

When it was over I was wheeled into the recovery room where two other Mums who had just given birth to two beautiful babies cooed with happiness. I desperately longed for my babies, and I had to turn my face away from the new Mums as they breastfed their little ones for the first time. I couldn't even hold my babies, and I feared I never would. After a short time a Children's Acute Transport Service (CATS) team arrived to prepare the boys for the move from UCLH to GOSH. Just before the boys were set to be taken from us I was wheeled in alongside them to say goodbye. It was a very emotional moment. The room fell completely silent and all I could do was reach down and stroke my baby boys because there was no way I could get up to kiss them. An Imam came to bless the boys, and he and Azzedine prayed over our precious pair for a moment.

Saying goodbye was almost impossible. I tried to see the babies from where I was lying, but all I could see were these tiny heads and this tangled mess of tubes. Then, once again, I was alone and heartbroken, my babies gone. Everywhere I looked around me there were new babies, this new life, their soft cries mixing in with my own. I could hear the excitement emanating from the other parents, their laughter filling the room when it hurt me even to cry. The angry wound that snaked its way across my belly was a mere scratch compared with the depth of the wound that slashed my heart. My boys were joined; I was torn in half. No painkillers, no matter how strong, could numb that pain.

I begged Azzedine to go with Hassan and Hussein. He was divided, as he didn't want to leave my side, but I didn't want them to be alone. I ached for them: their smell, their soft downy black hair, their tiny moist hands. I wanted to hold them close to me and hear their rapid breath, and feel their little hearts beating for myself. Azzedine could see how distraught I was, so he agreed to leave me and travel with the boys. I was alone for about an hour, when suddenly I heard my father's voice. The poor man had been desperately looking everywhere for me, but, as most of the staff had not been told about me, he had been unable to find me. Eventually our Cork midwife, Mary, had recognised his accent and brought him to me. I remember a look of relief flashed across his face when he saw me. He had been worried that he would lose his daughter. He sat by my side and was just there for me.

Later that day I texted some family and friends to say I was alive and that the boys were alive, for now, as I knew people at home were sick with worry. Eventually I was wheeled back to my own room, now a desolate, barren place. That precise moment had always been my favourite part of giving birth, when you finally got to be alone with your new precious baby. In one corner of the room stood a white, lonely cot, which, in its emptiness, seemed to almost mock me. I just lay there staring at it while the pain throbbed and burned across my body. I felt angry that I did not have a little bundle to put in it, that no happy blue balloons or congratulatory cards were there to greet me and fill my room with cheer. I had gone from being pregnant and full of life to this empty cot, this empty grey room of despair.

As if this wasn't enough, Azzedine came back to tell me that my boys were going to have to undergo surgery within the following 48 hours to rectify a blockage. I couldn't believe this. I just didn't think I could take any more bad news. I was terrified that I would lose them before I had even had a chance to hold them. Later that evening, there was a rap on my door and I was relieved to see the welcome face of Mr Kiely from GOSH coming in. He had just dropped in to let me know that my boys were OK. He would have known that the boys' imminent surgery would really worry me. Even though it was a fairly routine procedure, I knew any kind of surgery carried a risk with such small babies. The fact that my boys were undergoing surgery when they had been six weeks premature filled me with dread. Mr Kiely talked me through what would happen and reassured me they had carried out this type of procedure many times before. For his kindness and understanding I will always be grateful.

The following morning I spoke to the girls by phone, and told them the babies were alive. They came to see me later that day; I remember the door burst open and Malika ran into the room full of excitement and expectation. She stopped dead when she saw the empty cot. She looked at me, her eyes widening, and asked me where her brothers were. Her bottom lip began trembling as she asked, 'Mummy, are they dead?' Her words felt like daggers in my heart. Choking back my own tears I reassured my little girl that her baby brothers were alive, but had been taken away to another hospital so the doctors could help them grow stronger. I told her she would see them very soon. I don't think she fully believed me that they were alive. Part of me wanted her to go and see them, to see for herself that they had made it, but Azzedine did not want anybody seeing the babies before me. Poor Malika worried so much during my pregnancy, and now that they were born, she was still worried that they hadn't made it.

I desperately just wanted us all to be together, to get each other through this as a family. The fact that I didn't really have a clear image in my mind of what my boys looked like really bothered me. I remember asking Azzedine, 'When you close your eyes, and think of the boys, do you know what they look like?' to which he replied, 'Of course I do.' I cried as I explained to him that no matter how hard I tried, I couldn't get a clear picture of them in my mind. I didn't know what my own baby boys looked like! That tiny glimpse I had after they were born was not enough. Their faces were bloated with tubes and I barely got to see them anyway from where I was lying. I wanted to know every curve and line of their angelic faces. I wanted to hold their hands and feel the softness of their skin. I longed to see them when I closed my eyes. I squeezed my eyes shut and tried desperately to remember that fleeting moment I had got with them in the hospital when they were born. I remember seeing the skin joined across their chest and thinking how perfect they were despite their complications. You might think that conjoined babies are going to look strange or abnormal, but they were just beautiful, not strange at all—the more beautiful because of their precious drawing of breath.

The following day one of the nurses realised I had an empty cot in my room, which, mercifully, she discreetly took away. Although my boys were born on a Wednesday, 2 December, by Friday, I still had not seen them. They were the longest, most agonising, blackest days of my life. I was at UCLH and my boys were at GOSH. Azzedine would leave the flat in the morning to visit them, and then come to UCLH to visit me. He decided to take some photos for me, so I could see my babies, and I cried my heart out when I saw them. All during this time I was expressing milk for the boys, which Azzedine would then take over to UCLH. I cannot convey the depths of my despair when my milk production started to inexplicably dry up. The medics put it down to my not having had any skin-to-skin contact with the babies coupled with the trauma of the situation and the scale of the surgery I had undergone. I remember just crying and crying over a breast pump having produced this pathetic dribble of milk. So in the end they had to feed the boys with formula. I felt as if someone had stabbed me in the heart when I heard this. I had always breastfed my children. I had fed the two girls up to two years of age. There is nothing more natural than feeding your baby with your own milk, knowing you are giving them the best possible start in life. Now here were my boys, who had already had so much going against them, and I was unable to feed them. I felt immense guilt, disappointment and frustration that I could not provide this start for them. I felt as if I had let them down. I tried everything from medication to various homeopathic remedies to stimulate it but nothing worked. I kept trying for months, even when we were back in Cork, but it never came back. The nurses told me that I was being too hard on myself, and to just give it up as I cried over various breast pumps, but it absolutely killed me. It broke my heart too that Azzedine was getting to see the boys every day and I wasn't. Even though I got to see my lovely daughters, there was a huge, twins-shaped hole in my heart. I ached for them with every fibre of my being.

I hated that the boys were hooked up to loads of machines, lonely, without their Mummy. When I had my two girls I remember the rush of love and the immediate bonding after they were born and put to my breast, but these little children were taken away from me. I was so desperate for some contact with them that I came up with a plan. Before they were born I had bought each of my boys a blanket, even though they needed only one. I always made sure I got two of everything for them from the very beginning, as it was important to me that people realised they were two individuals. I organised, through Azzedine, that one of their blankets be sent over to me. I spent my nights with that blanket wrapped around me so I could smell their wonderfully warm baby scent. My body physically ached for them; there was no pain like it. Imagine giving birth and not being able to see or hold your child, day after endless day? Azzedine then took my blanket over to the boys so they might know their mother's scent, and this did comfort me a little.

I saw a massive change in Azzedine during this time. Because I was unable to leave my bed, he took over my role. He was the one going to all the meetings about the babies, and sorting out the paperwork, which I would have traditionally done. He had become a very hands-on Dad to these two little babies who had many complications. Kati Grey, our clinical psychotherapist, accompanied Azzedine to all these meetings, even on her days off, and she would report back to me what was said. Because I was in a country where I didn't know anyone, it was such a relief to have someone as kind and reliable as Kati by our side.

I was pining so much for my boys that I felt as if I were deteriorating rather than recovering. The nurses at UCLH saw how much I was suffering and came to my aid. They contacted the people at GOSH to find if there was any way I could see the babies, as they knew that my not being with them was killing me. They managed to convince them to let me go over to visit the boys, and so it was decided that I would be transported from UCLH to GOSH on Saturday, 5 December. I wasn't really well enough to travel as I was in such severe pain, but I didn't care: I was going to see my boys! My pain level was being continually monitored and, despite all the painkillers, it never let up: this constant, throbbing, burning agony that kept me awake every night. I could not use the bathroom, or get out of bed, and the staples pinched me all the time. I was on a cocktail of extremely strong painkillers, the doses of which were being constantly either upped or lowered. It was a most excruciating pain; it felt as if my whole stomach were still hanging open and parts of it had been dragged back together. I remember making a joke that in years to come the boys and I would be comparing battle scars, but I knew they were going to win hands down. When the news finally came through that I could go and see them, it felt amazing. I forgot all about my pain. I felt like a child on Christmas morning.

That Saturday, I asked the hospital staff to help me into a wheelchair so I could have a shower. I was determined to make myself look nice for these newborns, which was probably a little silly as they wouldn't be able to see me anyway! I was unbelievably excited that I was going to see them. I had longed so much for their smell, for the feel of their skin, and finally it was going to happen. A nurse accompanied me on the journey across by ambulance, and I could tell she was very excited for me. I remember the ambulance driver avoiding every bump and pothole on the road to cause me the least amount of pain. I was loaded up with morphine and painkillers before I left but I remember literally having to hold on to myself in the ambulance as I was in great pain. In hindsight I was so weak I probably shouldn't have gone anywhere, but the desire to see them was strong and overshadowed everything else.

I was wheeled off the ambulance and in the doors of GOSH, butterflies fluttering in my stomach the closer we got to the Neonatal Intensive Care Unit (NICU). I recalled the last time I was at this hospital and the sheer force of the devastating news that my boys had only one leg each; and now here I was, back again, and this time my boys were here with us. My father accompanied us so he could film those special first moments for us. I was taken aback by the level of security around the NICU, and how strange it was that Azzedine was very familiar with all these things that were quite alien to me. As we neared the boys' room, Azzedine began talking me through everything; he knew all the boys' carers by name, and which machine did what. Finally we were outside the boys' room. I had to take a few deep breaths before we went in. I thought I would explode with excitement. I was about to see my precious boys at last. I was going to meet my 'Little Fighters'.

Chapter 6

MEETING MY LITTLE FIGHTERS

The nurses smiled at me as I was wheeled past them and alongside the boys' bed. It felt strange being taken to see your own children for the first time, being surrounded by people who had already been caring for them for days without you. I barely knew what they looked like. My heart sank when I realised their bed was far too high for me to see into. What I could see were machines and wires, and it frightened me at first to see all those flashing monitors. I knew what I had to do, so, very slowly, I pulled myself up from my wheelchair to stand over my boys' bed. As excruciating as the pain was, I knew I had to see them. The last time I had caught a glimpse of them they were attached to a ventilator, these awful green tubes like plastic snakes in their mouths, bloating their tiny faces, making it almost impossible to see what they looked like. Now they were off the ventilation, and I was finally standing over my precious angels, my heart and soul, my beauteous, miraculous little boys. I cried at their gorgeous skin, the colour of honey; their precious arms wrapped around one another; their newborn eyes bright with life. I burst into tears from the relief of finally being with them. It was overwhelming. I struggled to keep my head above the river of emotion that had swept over me.

Our wedding day,
8 September 1999.

Me with Buddy on Youghal beach, 10
weeks pregnant and feeling so happy.
This photo was taken two weeks
before our first scan, which revealed I
was carrying conjoined twins.

Our first scan on 2 July 2009, which showed I was carrying conjoined twins.

Iman and me; I'm five months pregnant with Hassan and Hussein, 10 September 2009.

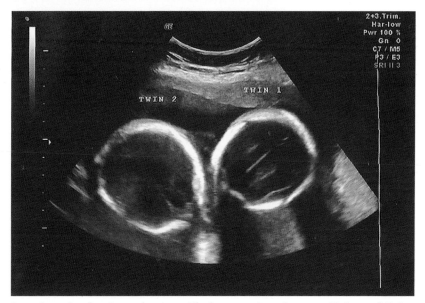

Scan photo dated 18 September 2009. The boys are given the names Twin 1 and Twin 2. Hassan is Twin 1; Hussein is Twin 2.

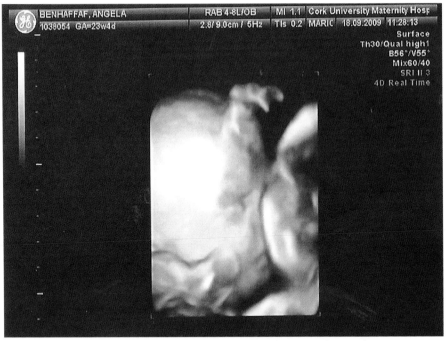

18 September 2009. The scan showed Hassan and Hussein kissing in the womb.

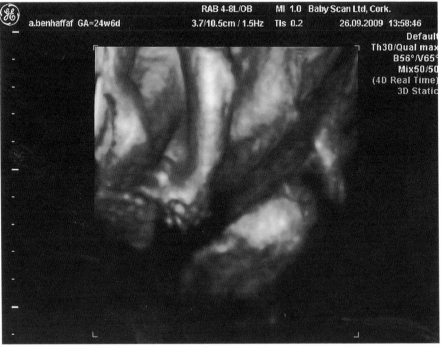

A 3D scan on 26 September 2009, which miraculously showed the boys clasping each other's hands in my womb. This was my picture of HOPE.

Malika and Iman at home, 20 September 2009, celebrating Eid.

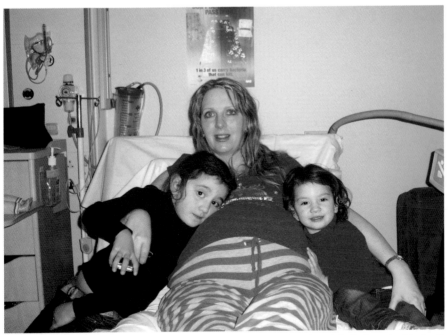

1 December 2009: Me with Malika and Iman at UCLH, London, the night before the birth of Hassan and Hussein.

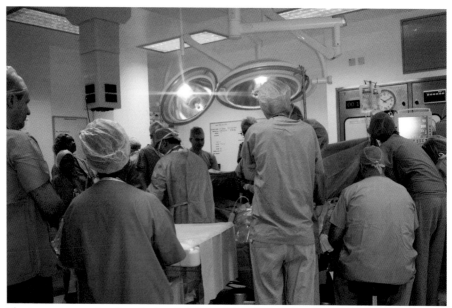

The team at UCLH, London, during the birth of Hassan and Hussein, 2 December 2009.

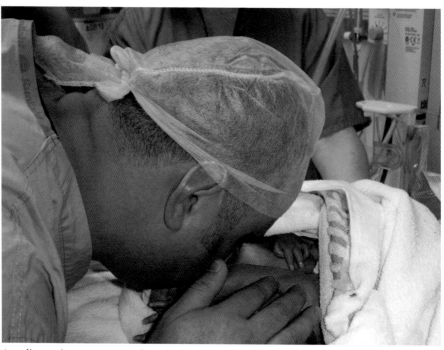

Azzedine saying prayers over the twins just after their birth, 2 December 2009.

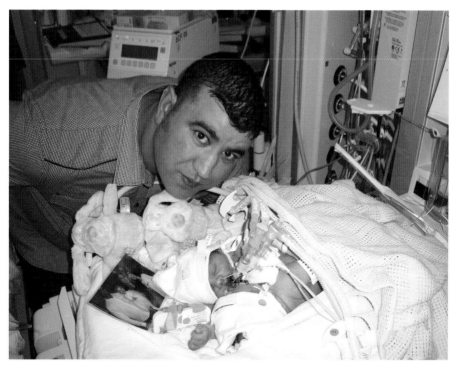

Azzedine with the boys after they were ventilated, 2 December 2009.

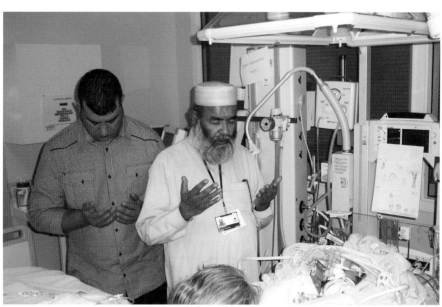

Azzedine with the Imam praying for the boys after their birth, with me watching. See Malika's picture attached to the cot. She drew her own picture of hope, which showed her with her two brothers holding hands and happy.

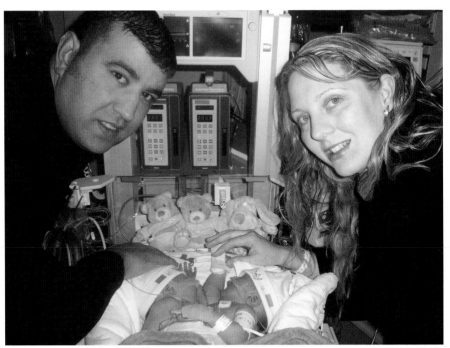

The first time I saw the twins since their birth. Pictured with Azzedine at GOSH, London, 5 December 2009.

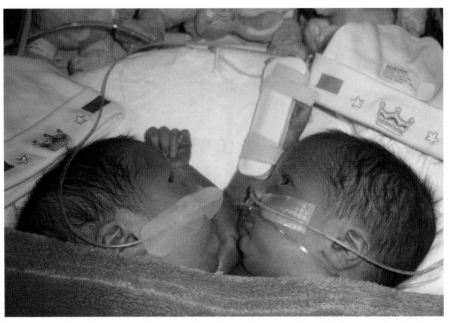

Hassan and Hussein at GOSH, three days old, 5 December 2009. See their 'PRINCE' motif hats, which represent the meaning of their names: Hassan means 'Prince', and Hussein means 'Handsome Prince'.

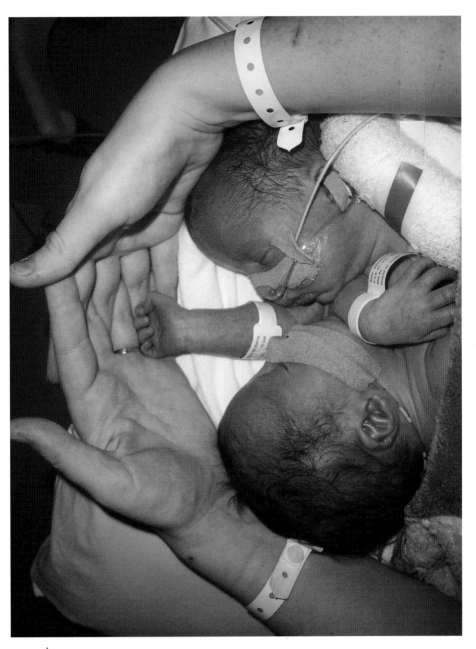

The Little Fighters, in my arms, one week old, 9 December 2009.

Me tenderly kissing the twins, nine days old, at GOSH, London, 11 December 2009. This was the morning after I got out of UCLH. (© *Medical Illustrations Great Ormond Street Hospital NHS Trust*)

Hassan and Hussein, nine days old at GOSH, London, 11 December 2009. (© *Medical Illustrations Great Ormond Street Hospital NHS Trust*)

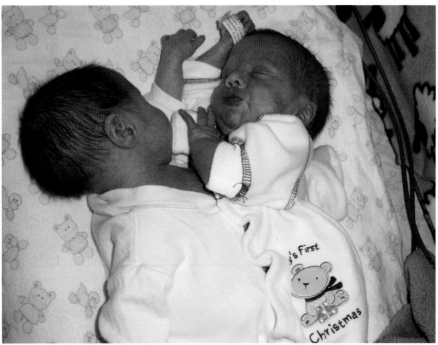

The boys back in CUMH, Cork, 17 days old, 19 December 2009.

Hassan and Hussein doing well at CUMH, Cork, 19 December 2009.

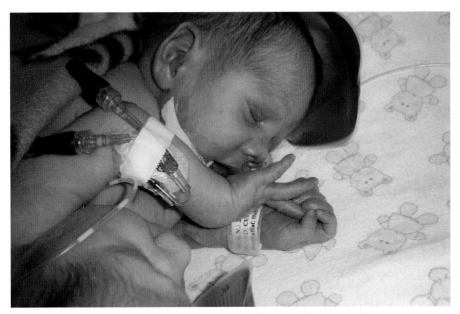

Hassan and Hussein fighting to survive, but clasping fingers still, 21 December 2009 at CUMH, Cork.

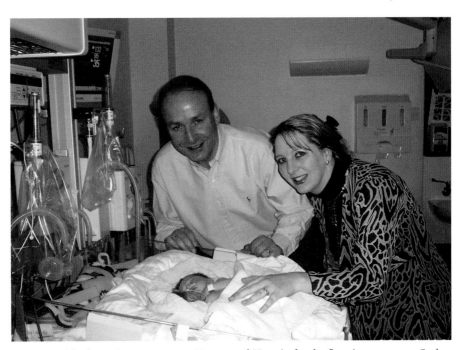

Minister Micheál Martin came to meet Hassan and Hussein for the first time at CUMH, Cork, 23 December 2009.

Malika with her brothers, Christmas Day 2009.

Iman with her brothers, Christmas Day 2009.

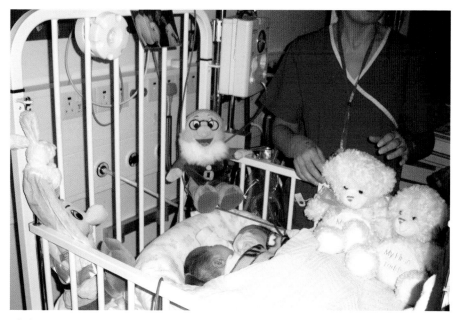

Christmas morning 2009 at CUMH, Cork; Santa has been!

The Christmas ornament I bought before the twins' birth to hang on our Christmas tree every year, in case they didn't survive. It would be our way of remembering them both every Christmas. Hassan on the left, Hussein on the right, as they were!

11 January 2010 at CUMH,
Cork.

All through my pregnancy I wondered what my boys would look like; sometimes society's version of what is considered normal would come rushing into my mind, and I would find myself worrying that perhaps they would look too different, and would suffer because of it, but on seeing them, I realised that I had never seen two babies look more beautiful. I knew them at that moment for the angels they were. I couldn't believe they had come off the ventilation within just 48 hours. They truly were my Little Fighters, both in name and spirit! Just two tiny tubes called CPAPS were going down their noses to assist with their breathing now. I leant over to kiss them, and the smell of them was like a burst of sudden life in my veins. I said, 'Hello, my angels, I'm your Mummy.' It felt wonderful to be with them, to be with my boys at last. I had ached for this moment.

After a few minutes the pain of standing became so overwhelming I thought I would pass out. The nurses, noticing my struggle, brought over a small, two-seater sofa for me to sit on. One of them smiled at me and uttered the words I had been longing to hear from the moment my boys were born: 'Would you like to hold your babies?' I couldn't believe I was going to get this opportunity on my first visit. I nodded while wiping away tears of joy. One of the nurses carefully lifted the boys out of their bed, while another nurse moved all their monitors and wires around to where I was sitting. Then, finally, I held my golden boys. It felt as if time stood still as I took them in my arms. My tears fell on their dark, sleeping heads as I cradled them close to me, something I never thought I would get a chance to do. I had prayed for this moment; I had imagined it many times, over and over in my head, this gorgeous dream of mine. I had told myself every day that they were going to live, and I was going to get to hold them, kiss them, smell them, but right until that joyous moment I don't know if I ever truly believed it. I had lain, torn apart, in that empty room for three long days and three endless nights just wanting to go to them, wondering if they would make it through, my pillow wet from my hot tears.

Throughout my pregnancy I had questioned why I was being punished with conjoined twins, but now I finally understood: this was no punishment; this was an amazing, wonderful gift. I knew we were chosen to be their parents, and it felt like such an honour to be their mother. My feelings changed utterly in that wondrous moment. They were my babies, no matter what they shared. I loved every single bit of them as they lay there in my arms, my sleeping babes. All of a sudden, Hassan woke up and the look of his beautiful newborn eyes filled me with happiness. I noticed the lovely heart shape their bodies made, and I loved them even more. I was happy that their join was at the chest, rather than anywhere else, and that they were holding each other and facing each other the way they were. I liked that they could see one another, help each other along.

It wasn't long before I started to feel quite weak and began to involuntarily slouch over the babies as the pain, despite the strength of the painkillers, racked my body. I tried to hide it from Azzedine and the nurses, but they soon noticed my distress. It was so hard to leave my boys. I dreaded returning to that empty room, which had no baby's cries to fill its vacuum. I couldn't bear to leave them; I had never been apart from my daughters and yet here were these newborns, struggling to stay alive, and I was to be parted from them again! I cried my heart out as I kissed them and let the nurse take them away. I sobbed all the way back to the ambulance, an agonising pain beginning to envelope me. By the time I got to my room, I was in such a bad way, I could hardly breathe, but it was nothing compared with the pain I felt being parted from my children. The doctors had to come and inject me with morphine and give me more painkillers. I paid for the visit that night. I knew I had pushed myself too hard because I wanted so desperately to be with them, but I also knew it had been worth every second of that painful, sleepless night. I made up my mind that night to get strong and mobile, to get out of that hospital bed to where my boys were. They needed me.

From the very next day I began to get out of bed at various intervals during the day and shuffle in and out of the bathroom, or anywhere I could, to try to show the doctors that I was getting stronger, and could soon be discharged. The nurses warned me to take it easy. I wasn't sleeping a lot; I felt like hell, but I had to get up, get to Hassan and Hussein. So few people knew about the twins at UCLH that one day, while I was shuffling around my bed, a nurse came into my room and asked me where my baby was. I had to say that I had given birth prematurely, and my baby was in another part of the hospital. It hurt to have to lie about my precious boys, but I just didn't have the energy to share our secret with anybody else.

I spent 11 longs nights in UCLH and on the twelfth day, Thursday, 10 December, I asked to be discharged. I knew my place was with my babies. It wasn't enough seeing them every other day, as a Mum I needed to be there with them all the time. I needed them to hear my voice, so they would know I was there. To my delight the doctors agreed to discharge me. Azzedine had found some new accommodation with a lift, as I could not manage to climb any stairs. The night I was discharged I went straight to the new apartment and waited for my girls to come home. They were very excited. Malika kept asking me whether I was home for good, while Iman squealed with delight. That night the girls insisted on sleeping in the single bed with me. I was nervous they would upset my wound, but it did feel good to sleep nestled into my little girls once again.

The next morning I got up when it was still dark outside. It was bitterly cold; a thick blanket of sparkling white snow lay all around, enchanting, like Christmas morning. I threw my furry coat on over my pyjamas and slippers and set off for the hospital. I remember my Aunt Val laughing at me, and telling me that I couldn't go out dressed that way, but I didn't care. I was going over to those boys, and I was going to visit them on my own.

I decided that morning that I wanted to get a family portrait done after my visit. I had been told that GOSH had their own photographic studio, where families with sick children could go to have their portrait taken, so I made arrangements for us all to come by later that day. I went home and put the girls in their best dresses, dressed myself, and asked Azzedine to put on a nice shirt. I asked Val to go out to buy some babygrows. I knew she was wondering how I would manage to get them on the twins, but I was tired of my poor babies being naked all the time. I wanted them to be dressed and warm. Val returned with a three-pack of babygrows so I took the tiny little suits out of the packaging and just stared at them for a while, wondering how I would get them on the babies. Suddenly it struck me that if I press fastened one babygrow to the other, I could get them on the pair of them. I got more creative as time went by. I often used to joke that Hassan and Hussein would be the world's best-dressed conjoined twins, as they always looked adorable. When I dressed them I tried my best to make sure they wore two completely different patterns or colours, to let people know they were two individuals, with two distinct personalities. I felt I had to present them to the world like that, so people would realise just how distinct they were from one another. I packed the babygrows in a bag, got the family together, and set off for the hospital to proudly pose for our family photo.

The boys were wheeled down with their oxygen supply and handed to me. I had to kneel down with them for the shot and I remember the pain I felt trying to get back up afterwards, but it was worth it—the photographs were lovely. I know conjoined twins may seem different to some people, but to us they were our perfect little boys. I loved those photos; they represented just how far we had come as a family since this news first exploded into our lives.

———

As the days ran on I took on more and more of the boys' care. I wanted to learn each and every thing I could to care for them myself. At the beginning I did get upset sometimes; I had two babies but just one nappy, and sometimes when I looked at them while I was changing them I would feel sad. I was worried for them, but in the end they are your beautiful babies, so you just love them the way they are.

The boys had been in the NICU ward for the best part of two weeks when we were informed they were well enough to be moved on to a surgical ward. Their oxygen support had been reduced considerably, which was amazing. They had been born six weeks premature, and coupled with that they were conjoined and had undergone surgery in the first 48 hours of their lives, but they were thriving, and coping well with their feeds. They looked really healthy and handsome. I had grown to love how they looked, and couldn't imagine them being any other way. To me they were completely special and wondrous. Iman was so young at the time that she did not notice anything different about her brothers, but I would watch Malika's eyes examining every part of them. I worried that it would upset her that they were different, but it never did; she absolutely adored them. Sometimes she would say, 'Mam, I wish the brothers had two legs each.' I knew that really saddened her, and I remember telling her that her little brothers would do everything she could do and one day they would get pretend legs and walk hand in hand with her and Iman. I could see in her eyes how she longed for that day to come.

On 11 December, Azzedine and I were brought into a room to be given an update on the boys' condition, a meeting we had been very nervous about. We were both scared about what was coming; after all, we had gone into meetings like this in the past and left them devastated. We were both really worried that there would be bad news for our boys. We felt like frightened children as Prof Pierro and Mr Kiely came in with key members of the boys' team. The room fell silent as Mr Kiely began to speak, and my stomach lurched. He reassured us that the boys were doing very well, and we were in fact going to be able to take them home soon so they could grow and put on weight. He then told us he hoped the boys would be able to return to the hospital to undergo separation surgery on 7 April 2010. We were not expecting this at all. Obviously I knew separation surgery was on the cards, but I had no idea it would be that soon. I remember just blurting out that was the date the boys had been conceived and Mr Kiely laughingly responded, 'Well, we didn't need to know that!' Everybody laughed as colour rose in my cheeks. We had planned the pregnancy so carefully that I was very much aware of the date my boys were conceived. I thought it was such a strange coincidence that they were going to be separated exactly one year on from the day they were created.

From the beginning we were told there was still a chance they would not be suitable for separation, and 7 April was always just a provisional date. In fact, right up until the very day before the boys' surgery took place, we didn't know if it would even go ahead, which was difficult. I pictured my boys holding hands in the womb and through all the desperate fear I decided to look at it as them getting a chance to be created again. It was an impossibly difficult decision allowing the surgery to go ahead. The longer we got to know them the more normal they appeared to us: they were my babies who were joined together. To see them apart would be very peculiar. I loved the little bones of them in their bundle of love, arms slung around one another, and their cries, which always started and stopped simultaneously as if some tiny conductor was controlling them. If I had followed my heart then I would have left them in their sweet embrace together forever, but I had to follow my head. I knew I had to give them a chance at life. They were gorgeous little babies now, but they wouldn't be babies for long. Soon they would be boys, then teenagers and finally men. I knew what we had to do.

——

As the weeks went by the boys continued to thrive, and we could hardly believe our luck. Despite our happiness, however, we were terrified that they were leaving the NICU ward to move to a general surgical ward. In normal circumstances parents would be jumping for joy that their babies were considered well enough to leave an intensive care unit, but our happiness was tainted by fear. There was such tight security around us at the NICU ward; we felt safe and secure there: nobody could get into that ward without being buzzed in. We were frightened that in this new ward there would be other staff and other families around who might see the boys, and our secret would get out. We didn't know how it was going to be possible to keep our presence there quiet. I also felt very sad saying goodbye to the amazing staff who had cared for our babies so well. They had seen us through an extremely difficult period, and we had grown very close to them.

When we arrived at the Woodland Ward at GOSH, I was relieved to see the boys had their own room. We protectively drew the curtains around them in case anyone looked in. I was already tired of the secrecy and having to hide them all the time, but at least our secret was safe for now. Cleaning staff would sometimes just wander into the boys' room to empty the bins and things, and I remember the terror I would feel that they would realise the babies were conjoined. I was always trying to cover them up, instinctively protecting them from the wolves that were beginning to circle.

There were some amazing pluses to the boys being out of the high dependency unit; one was being able to feed them ourselves. We started off with one bottle each—one for Hassan and one for Hussein—and Azzedine and I would take turns to feed them. It was like a game of Twister sometimes, crossing your hands over and back as they hungrily drank. I remember thinking how their big brown eyes, like pools of innocence, would melt the hardest of hearts. It took some degree of skill to pull off feeding time, and sometimes my hands would ache from it, but it soon got easier. I went into them day after day with the belief that anything was possible for my children: they would be as happy as any other child; they would be fed, loved and cherished; they would be dressed and warm; they would laugh and run and play and be free. I knew, as their mother, I had to believe in this dream for my boys. The very fact that they were alive and there with us was proof enough that dreams, no matter how seemingly impossible, do come true.

We were in the new ward for only a few days when the hospital's head of communications, Stephen Cox, came to speak to us. I remember being truly stunned as he told us that some media organisations, such as Sky News, TV3 in Ireland and the *Daily Star* newspaper, were making calls to the hospital saying a source in Ireland had revealed how a pair of conjoined twins had been born in London to an Irish mother. I was absolutely gobsmacked. I didn't know what to do. We were dumbfounded. We asked ourselves over and over how they could possibly know this. Who had told them about our precious boys? I felt a creeping fear run down my spine. I just couldn't believe there were strangers phoning up, trying to get information about our little babies. I was worried about the twins, and how the media would portray them, and I was still so ill from my own operation that I just couldn't have coped if it had come out. The hospital was refusing to respond to the media enquiries, so we knew nothing would be printed straight away; but I also knew that it would only be a matter of time. I was later told that the maternity hospital in Cork had also been receiving calls. It felt like the world was closing in on us, pressing down on our little family.

Stephen explained to us that we had a number of options, and suggested we possibly might need an agent. I remember thinking how bizarre a concept that was. We were an ordinary family with twin babies who just happened to be conjoined. I could not understand why this would mean I needed an agent! It was only after the boys' story hit the headlines that I understood why. Nothing could have prepared us, a normal, everyday family, for the extent of the worldwide interest in our boys. Malika used to often ask me why everybody was fussed about the babies. 'They are just stuck together, Mummy!' she would say, a bemused expression on her face, but to the world's media they were of huge interest. We knew that male conjoined twins were extremely rare, so there would be a bit more hype around them, but we had no idea just how much attention they would generate. So there we were, in this surgical ward full of twinkling Christmas decorations, and outside the media was beginning to push in. I remember feeling paranoid that someone would come into the hospital posing as a visitor to try to get information. It was a horrible feeling.

———

Slowly but surely, Christmas began to make its way into my peripheral vision as we kept a 24-hour vigil at the boys' bedside, Azzedine and I taking it in turns to stay with them. I recall one day there was this huge commotion on the ward, and when we stepped outside the boys' room to see what was going on, we were greeted by all these Disney characters running about. There was a special Christmas visit organised for the kids at the hospital. The girls ran out full of excitement to enjoy the party. It felt lovely just to see them excited and happy, their gorgeous smiles outshining the twinkling fairy lights. Suddenly, this 7 ft Goofy character appeared in our room. Instinctively I rushed to cover the twins. I felt panicked that a stranger was going to see them, but then, I just decided to relax. I didn't think that someone who would come and spend a day trying to make things easier for sick children was someone I needed to worry about. I still have this lovely photograph of Goofy bending over my boys and stroking them on the cheek. We were nervous, but we also felt happy to have a quick slice of normality. The boys looked tiny next to this giant colourful character.

Mr Kiely was calling in to check on the boys every day, and he was very happy with their progress. Then, one afternoon, about 10 days before Christmas, he came to see us and told us that Hassan and Hussein were no longer sick enough to stay in GOSH; they could go home to Cork. This was such wonderful news in one respect, because, as parents, you want your child to be well with every drop of blood in your body, but at the same time the prospect of taking them home terrified us. GOSH had become this little cocoon where we were wrapped in cotton wool. We felt safe there; the boys were safe there. Time and place ceased to have any real relevance as we watched over that precious cargo night and day. It had been three weeks since their birth and it had still not broken in the media. Now we started to panic and ask ourselves how we would be able to keep this quiet in Cork where we knew so many people. How were we going to be able to leave the house? The thought of going home was an extremely daunting prospect.

| RETURNING HOME TO CORK

I had been walking around in a fog since the twins' birth—my days consisted of going from the flat to the hospital and back again. Days passed into night and into day again as I watched, waited and prayed at my children's bedside, waiting in a vacuum of uncertainty. It was only when plans for our return home were finalised that it began to sink in that we were going to arrive back in Cork a few days before Christmas and I had nothing ready. The nursery wasn't even ready for the boys. I just couldn't bring myself to prepare it before we left in case we lost the babies. I knew it would have crushed me to arrive home distraught and bereft to that baby-blue coloured empty nest. We had had no idea when, or even whether, we would be coming home with our babies, and we certainly never envisaged it happening by Christmas. I had no Christmas tree for the house, nor any presents for the girls.

What worried me even more was the fact that the boys were coming home to be admitted into yet another hospital where we would once again have to worry what kind of level of privacy or security we would have. In a hospital in my hometown, I could easily walk into someone I knew in its corridors. I had built up an enormous sense of trust with the staff at GOSH. We felt safe there;

our secret was safe there; so the thought of all of us being sent home was not the joyful celebration I had initially imagined it to be. Of course, I was thinking about the positive sides too. After all, we were all going back to Cork. Our girls would be safely back in their home for Christmas where I knew they longed to be. Malika would be delighted to be reunited with her friends, but there was no escaping the fact that the prospect of going home was also hugely daunting.

I had called Minister Martin to tell him we were coming home and, through him and the hospital, plans were put in place for our transfer to Cork Airport. He reassured me that a private cubicle had been set up for the boys in the neonatal unit of CUMH where they would be as safe and secure as they had been in the UK. We were to travel out of London City Airport by air ambulance in a matter of days after which I was going to travel to CUMH with the boys, while Azzedine would take the girls home.

We packed up all our things with a mixture of dread and excitement. It was such a strange feeling as neither Azzedine nor I actually wanted to go home; we just didn't want to leave GOSH. We were removed from our home life, and living in a kind of bubble from which I was afraid to emerge. I didn't want to have to meet new people and new doctors, nor did I want to have to depend on these new people to keep our precious secret. I was afraid of reporters finding out we were back in Cork. I hated having to hide my wonderful babies—this gorgeous pair who had fought hard for life—but we had no choice.

We woke the morning of departure to find a heavy blanket of snow had fallen silently over London. I pulled my sleepy daughters from their beds and got them ready. A CATS team had been working since first light to prepare Hassan and Hussein for the journey, so we gathered up our things for the last time and headed over to the hospital. When we arrived, they were putting the boys into what looked like a space capsule to keep them safe from infection during the journey. As we waited for the go-ahead with our suitcases, prams and baggage, we said some tearful goodbyes to the staff at GOSH. We had grown close to the people at that hospital and it was very hard to say goodbye.

Finally it was time to go. I remember the cold air stung my face and I could see my breath like smoke on the frozen air. I pulled my coat collar tighter and climbed onboard the ambulance to embark on the next stage of our journey. As the ambulance pulled out onto the road, I looked back at the hospital and thought it would not be long before we were back there again facing another torturous challenge. We were on the road only a few minutes when one of the drivers decided to contact London City Airport to see if it was all systems go. I remember feeling really frustrated when we were told that conditions were too poor for take-off, so we had to turn back to the hospital. It had taken quite a lot to say goodbye to the staff, and to leave that safe haven. I didn't want to have to go back through those doors, but in we went. We hung around the ward for a couple of hours feeling nervous and full of trepidation until we eventually got the all-clear from the airport.

The staff at GOSH told us there would be an ambulance, a doctor and a nurse waiting to meet us at Cork Airport and that all the staff in the Cork neonatal ward had been briefed about the fact that the presence of our babies there was to be highly confidential, so I tried to relax on the journey. They were also warned that there would be serious repercussions if our boys' presence there became public knowledge. We finally arrived at London City Airport's runway where a tiny air ambulance was waiting for us. As the plane took off, I felt very anxious. As we chugged through the clouds I looked at my girls chattering to one another and thought how utterly changed our lives now were.

Eventually, we touched down in Cork Airport and emerged from the plane to a cold December morning: ice underfoot and fear in my heart. We were met by the team from CUMH. Our nurse from GOSH prepared to hand over the boys as I kissed the girls goodbye and told them they were going home with Daddy. There was a private taxi on the runway, ready to take Azzedine and the girls back to Carrigtwohill. Just as I was getting ready to get into the ambulance, one of the personnel told me I wasn't permitted to travel with my boys as there was no room. I couldn't believe this. I really didn't want to leave their side. I felt very protective towards them. I told Azzedine that they wouldn't allow me in so he tried to intervene on my behalf. He told the ambulance driver that we had been given assurances that I would be able to travel with the boys, that I was frightened for them, but they just would not let me go with them. I had this idea in my head that if I didn't go with my sons, they could end up being examined and prodded at the hospital by people who were just trying to satisfy their own curiosity. But I knew this was just my imagination. The nurse who came to collect the boys from CUMH was Anne Buckley, who would be a special part of the boys' journey.

I could hear Azzedine getting increasingly agitated, so I walked over to see if I could talk to the ambulance driver myself. When I got around to his side I was absolutely shocked to discover that the driver was an old neighbour of mine, Seán O'Sullivan, whom I had grown up with! He looked at me in complete shock. Even though he was the one driving the ambulance, he had not been told what the issue was with the babies. All he had been told was to come and collect two babies from the airport to bring back to the hospital. He asked us to wait a moment while he boarded the plane to bring the babies off. When he re-emerged I could see his face had turned ashen and his hands were shaking. He said, 'Angie, I'm so sorry,' and told me I could travel in the front of the ambulance with him. Azzedine waved goodbye as he headed for home with the girls and I climbed in with my old neighbour and looked back at my boys.

We arrived at the neonatal unit at CUMH through a secret entrance. I remember walking into the unit and feeling quite light-headed and overwhelmed. There were all these other parents around and lots of staff. I surprised myself and the staff by bursting into tears a couple of minutes after we arrived. I was just emotionally exhausted; I had no idea what kind of system was in place there and I felt as if I had no control over what was going to happen to my boys.

I was brought into the private room where the boys were being examined by a team of doctors, and immediately became quite defensive. Obviously the doctors were just doing their job, but to my shaken mind everyone who came into that room was there only to have a look at them. My guard went up like a shield; I didn't trust anyone and I didn't want to leave the twins alone for any period of time. The doctors asked me to explain a little of their history to date, and my stress eased a little as I recounted everything I knew up to that point. Dr Peter Filan, the twins' doctor, came in to see them for the first time then. He just strolled in and looked at them and stroked their little faces and left again. A few moments later he came back into the room again and stood there smiling at them. I said, 'I know why you are smiling.' He looked at me bemused and asked, 'Why, what are you thinking?' So I replied, 'Isn't it because you were expecting these two sick babies, but what you see here before you are two beautiful boys, as healthy as you or I?' He laughed and I felt myself starting to relax.

Meanwhile, Azzedine arrived back to our dark, cold house feeling like a fugitive on the run with two little girls in tow. He hurriedly paid the taxi fare, gathered up the girls and our luggage, and ran into the house. He pulled down all the blinds. He was afraid to turn on any lights in the front of the house in case somebody noticed. We had agreed that if anybody called, he wouldn't answer the door. We had not told anyone in advance we were coming home, and that was how we had planned to keep it. Secrecy was the only way we could ensure our boys were protected. The last thing we wanted was to arrive home to a gaggle of media outside the door, waiting for us with their questions and their cameras. There was absolutely nothing in the house, no milk, no bread—nothing. The girls were complaining about being hungry, but Azzedine was afraid to leave because he knew our neighbours and friends would see him, and the first thing they would ask would be whether I had my babies.

That evening I called my Aunt Val from the hospital to see if she would bring me home but I was unable to get through, so I tried my cousin's wife, Sinead. She picked up immediately. I told her I had something huge to tell her and needed her help. I said I was at CUMH and asked if she could come and get me. She had flown to London to see the twins when they were born, so I was very close to her; in fact, she, Val and my father were the only ones who had actually seen Hassan and Hussein in the flesh. There was a pause at the end of the line as she, completely confused, tried to take in what I had just said. She half shouted, 'Oh my God, Angie, why are you in Cork?' She was worried something had happened to the babies. I did feel bad that I had alarmed her so much, but I needed her help as I couldn't drive. I was still in quite a significant amount of pain from my surgery and I couldn't risk getting behind the wheel. In fact, I had been told it would take a whole year for my wounds to fully heal. I hung up the phone and within minutes Sinead and my cousin Brendan jumped in the car and drove straight up to the hospital. We had quite a tearful reunion in the car park.

We decided to head straight for a 24-hour Tesco in Wilton to get some supplies for my house. Before we went into the supermarket I was trying to change my appearance in the back of the car by tying up my hair. I had grown up in that area of Cork and I really didn't want to meet anyone. I simply didn't have the energy for it. Once inside, we scurried around the store, throwing completely useless items in the trolley. I tried not to notice all the sparkling Christmas decorations and the relentless chirp of festive music in the background. I was worried for my children at home and I was worried for the pair back at the hospital. My mind was just racing. It all felt very peculiar—being back in Cork and skulking around, trying not to be seen. We paid for the groceries and got out of the supermarket very quickly. My cousin dropped me home and I remember us all sitting around the kitchen table and how strange it felt that this wasn't the joyful homecoming that I imagined, but one shrouded in secrecy and tears.

The next day, while I was at the hospital with the boys, my brother Jason came to the house. He had been calling by intermittently while we were in the UK to check that things were OK. When he noticed a light on, he turned the key nervously, afraid that someone had broken in. He was stunned to discover his nieces and Azzedine standing in the living room. He couldn't believe they were home, but when he did not see me he panicked. Azzedine explained to him what had happened and so, slowly, more family and friends learned of our return. Before my father had a chance to find out I decided to surprise him. I phoned him up the following day and told him we had some documents for collection at the neo-natal unit in CUMH and asked if he would pick them up for me. I said a counsellor would meet him at the hospital at 2 p.m.; in the meantime I went out to the car park with the girls to wait for him. When he arrived at CUMH, we could see him walking up towards the hospital so we jumped out from behind a car. The poor man almost fainted from the shock! He was very happy that we were all home and I was more than glad to see him.

We went home that night to our own house in the bitter cold. Ice clung to everything. I hated leaving the boys. I really wanted to stay with them, but I knew it was important that I be there for my girls, who were obviously feeling a bit discombobulated by everything that had happened. That night I woke up in the early hours to the shrill sound of the house phone ringing. I pulled on my dressing gown and ran down the stairs. When I picked up the receiver it was the boys' specialist, Dr Filan. My stomach lurched as he told me I had to come to the hospital immediately: Hassan was very ill. I could not believe that within 24 hours of arriving home my baby was ill. My head started spinning as panic gripped me. I kept thinking how Hassan was always referred to as the stronger twin, so how could it be that he was sick now? I became quite hysterical on the phone. I saw on the wall clock that it was 6 a.m. To be woken to this news at that hour of the morning is every mother's worst nightmare. I begged Dr Filan to tell me how bad the situation was. 'Could he die?' I shouted down the phone. I felt like throwing up when Dr Filan said he couldn't answer that question.

That winter was one of the bitterest Ireland had experienced in many years. There was a sheet of thick ice on the road that morning, but in the state I was in I would have run across a bed of nails to get to my children. I knew I wasn't supposed to drive because of my wound, but I had to get to the hospital and Azzedine had to stay at home with the girls. I pulled a heavy coat over my pyjamas, threw on the first pair of boots my eyes fell upon, and then jumped into my little Yaris, as my heart thumped in my chest. I tried and tried the ignition, but it just rattled and died. I hadn't driven the car in a month; the cold and the ice had choked it. Later, Azzedine said he thanked God my car had not started that morning as I would almost certainly have had an accident.

I called my brother Jason and asked him to come and get me immediately. Jason lives in Midleton, which is only a few miles from Carrigtwohill, and even though he came for me straight away, I will never forget just how long the wait felt. When he pulled up outside my house I jumped into his car. I could barely speak I was crying so hard as we raced towards the hospital, the car slipping and sliding on the road in the dark. The only thought in my mind was how I couldn't lose my baby Hassan, not now, not after everything. Finally I saw the hospital looming ahead of us. I ran from the car park, trying my best not to slip and fall. The hospital was usually very strict about only allowing Mums and Dads into the neonatal unit, but I think they could see that I was barely able to stand with fear and panic, so they let Jason come in with me.

I remember walking into the boys' cubicle and wanting to scream. Hassan looked bad, very waxen and deathly. I heard Jason gasp beside me; not only was this his first time seeing them, but Hassan's pallor shocked him. Just a few hours previously I had left them in perfect health, thinking the two of them looked beautiful; the rosy pink colour in their cheeks was as reassuring as home. They had been lying in a regular cot in their cute babygrows looking sleepy and content. Everything was well with them; now they were stripped naked in the intensive care unit under those harsh lights with masks around their faces to aid their breathing. Hassan looked so yellow and ill that it chilled my blood to look at him; Hussein was a normal, healthy pink next to his pale and wan brother. What then happened before our very eyes I will never forget; the colour began to drain from Hussein's face and he began to take on his brother's waxen look while the colour returned to Hassan's cheeks. The illness was literally passing from one to the other and back again, mocking us with its lethal hue. Even the doctors present looked shocked.

I knew enough to know how badly this boded for both twins. I was painfully aware that if one conjoined twin becomes seriously ill, doctors can end up having to carry out an emergency separation to save the other twin. All this information was whirling around in my head as I helplessly stood by and watched this poison dance between my boys. I couldn't possibly imagine anything worse than one of my babies dying alongside the other, for one tiny baby to have to feel that kind of loss, that light going out beside him. I also knew there was a big chance that I would lose both twins if an emergency separation was carried out. I thought I would succumb to the waves of panic that slammed up against me relentlessly.

The doctors told me Hassan had tested positive for Septicaemia or blood poisoning, but what baffled them was that Hussein had tested negative. Terrified, I asked the doctors to tell me if they were going to die, but all they kept saying was it was too early to say. We were back in Ireland only 24 hours and already I was facing the possibility of losing my children. I kept thinking that I should never have taken them out of London. I could not stop crying and my body shook with fear. My brother looked pale; he didn't know if this would be his first and last time seeing his nephews. I know he tried to stay strong for me, but I could tell he was really frightened.

From that point on I refused to leave the boys' room. I didn't drink anything; I couldn't eat or sleep; I refused to leave their bedside. I remember getting down on my knees and begging God again and again to let my babies live, as hot, salty tears ran down my tired face. The neonatal team at CUMH were an amazing support. Lucille Bradfield, head sister at the neonatal unit, would just sit with me and tell me over and over that I would get through it, while another nurse, Anne Twomey, just chased me from morning to night trying to get me to eat or have a cup of tea. I will always remember their kindness, which helped me through what was a difficult time. I was terrified that I would lose one or both of my boys. The doctors decided to start them on a course of antibiotics; it was really just a shot in the dark, but thankfully, in true Little Fighters spirit, Hassan began to respond well quite quickly. I kept a vigil at their bedside as the colour slowly returned to their cheeks. It felt as if I hadn't drawn breath in days, the aching, agonising pain of watching your little one struggling, fighting for life. I would have gladly swapped places with him.

As they began to recover, I felt torn as I was aware of all the time I was spending in hospital and yet my two little girls were missing me. It was Christmas, so of course I wanted to be with my girls, but it seemed impossible to strike a balance between being the best possible mother I could to both my girls and my boys. Once the boys started to get out of danger I did begin to go home in the evenings but I literally lay on my bed in the dark and waited for the phone to ring with more devastating news. It was like that for days; I walked around in a haze of exhaustion until I was certain they were out of the woods.

One afternoon I was holding the boys and humming the Westlife song 'You Raise Me Up' to them when one of the boys' nurses asked me if I liked Westlife. I replied, 'Yes, that song gave me hope when I was pregnant and I always played it for the boys.' I also explained to her how the girls loved Michael Jackson's song 'You Are Not Alone' and how both songs took on a deep significance for us during my pregnancy. She then surprised me by telling me that the boys' specialist, Dr Filan, was in fact a brother of Westlife star Shane Filan! I laughed thinking she was joking, but at that moment Dr Filan walked into the boys' little secret hideaway. I looked at him and giggled. He asked me to share the joke. I told him I didn't believe he was Shane Filan's brother, to which he replied, 'No, no, Shane is *my* brother!' I felt this was another one of those lovely coincidences that followed my boys throughout their journey and made me believe that there was something incredibly special about them.

Chapter 8 ～

ANNOUNCING A VERY
SPECIAL BIRTH

I t was 23 December before the boys had completely recovered.
I remember waking that morning feeling hollow from
exhaustion, as if I had just emerged out of a thick, black fog. I
reached across to my bedside table and picked up a piece of paper
by my bed. It was a list Malika had written for Santa Claus with
her coloured crayons, which she had adorned with brightly
coloured kisses and stars. I felt sad as I read down through it. I
knew there was no way I could get any of the things she wanted at
that late stage: everything would be long sold out. I felt guilty.
After all, I was her mother. It was my job to protect her from
disappointed hopes. The boys had been so ill that we had focused
all our energy on them, willing them to pull through. Everything
else had been put on hold for those critical few days, but now the
reality of my girls not having any Christmas to speak of started to
really hit home. As hard as I tried I couldn't get anything on
Malika's list. Absolutely everything was sold out and I just couldn't
bear for my little girl to be let down.

The following morning, my friend Joan called to my house and
asked me to give her Malika's list. I was grateful and relieved that
somebody was going to help me, but sadly there was nothing to be

got. She tried suggesting alternative things that I could buy for her, but as she spoke, my mind raced with worry about what we could actually afford. The grim reality of our financial status made me feel unwell every time I thought about it. Azzedine had not worked in a month, so money was extremely tight. Finally, in a last ditch attempt at Christmas shopping, Joan and I decided to drive out to Smyths toy store on Christmas Eve. I bought the boys two blue teddies and the girls some small presents. I felt relieved that at least they would be waking up to find presents under the tree on Christmas morning after all. I knew Azzedine was put out by the fact that I was running around trying to sort everything out when I was still quite weak from my surgery. He thought I had put far too much pressure on myself to make things better for the children, but I felt as if I had failed them. Azzedine did not have a Santa Claus in his childhood in Algeria, and I don't think he realised just how important he is to children.

I remember my own childhood Christmas mornings: sneaking down the stairs in my pyjamas, the wondrous joy of finding those presents under the tree. I knew how crushed I would have been if I had come downstairs and found nothing there waiting for me. I also wanted my boys to wake up to find some presents, so later that day I went to the hospital and some of the nursing staff and I hid their presents until the morning. I knew the boys were far too small to know the difference, but it was such a momentous thing that they were alive and kicking and back in Cork for Christmas Day that I really wanted to mark it. The nurses gave me two wooden toys for the boys and a doll's house and desk and chair for the girls. I remember creeping into the boys' room with one of their nurses, Anne Buckley, like two excited children hiding their presents and whispering so we wouldn't wake them. She promised me she would come in later and put the gifts in the cot for them, then I bent over and kissed my boys goodnight. I went home in a panic, put up the Christmas tree that Azzedine had picked up earlier and wrapped the presents. I worked into the early hours, wanting everything to be as perfect as it could be.

I woke on Christmas morning to the girls' squeals of delight and felt my heart glow with happiness. They were absolutely delighted with what we had given them, which was typical of them—they never complained. I felt so happy that they were having a Christmas. Of course kids being kids, Malika's favourite thing was a tiny bouncing ball that had cost only a few cents. It was our most basic Christmas to date, but equally our best. I brought a present from the boys to the girls to make sure they felt connected to their little brothers and we enjoyed a gorgeous Christmas morning together.

A week before I travelled to London to have the babies I had come across a small Christmas decorations kiosk in a local shopping centre, which stocked gorgeous tree ornaments that could be engraved. As I was browsing, I spotted a decoration of two little teddies hugging one another. It reminded me so much of my little boys that I decided to buy it and have their names engraved on the trim of the teddies' blue Christmas hats. On Christmas morning I went upstairs and took it out of its box and brought it downstairs. We shared a wonderful family moment placing it on the tree together in honour of our Little Fighters. Coincidentally the lady at the kiosk had engraved Hassan's name on the left and Hussein's on the right, which was exactly how they were. I told her that my babies were not well and I wanted this to put on my Christmas tree so that if anything happened to them, it would be a way of remembering them every year on Christmas Day. I remember the feeling of joy I had watching those little teddies twinkling and twirling on our tree, dappled by light.

That afternoon all four of us headed up to the hospital to see our boys. I laughed when I noticed how much bigger the teddies I had chosen for them were than the babies! I picked up my boys, gave them a cuddle and wished them a Happy Christmas. I gave them a Christmas card just from me. In it I had written: *'To my darling Hassan and Hussein, I now understand that you were a gift, love Mummy.'* As I bent over them I thought about how it was Christmas Day, we didn't have much in our pockets, but we really had everything in the world. They were the most sacred of Christmas gifts, so unexpected, a true miracle of life. Throughout my pregnancy I had often thought about how that Christmas would be. I envisaged it being traumatic, full of sadness, loss and black despair, but instead it was full of happiness and delight. I took my boys in my arms and carried them secretly down to the family room where their sisters and Daddy were waiting for them. Malika and Iman kicked off their shoes and climbed up on the bed to play with them. We just stayed there for hours like that, together, the six of us—at last. It was truly the most perfect Christmas I have ever had. We had our beautiful sons; we could want for nothing more.

———

The twins spent a number of weeks in the neonatal ward in Cork and, as in London, we grew close to the staff there. They had also become very protective of the twins and I knew we did not have to worry about it getting out, but I also knew it was time to take the plunge, and let it be known that they were in the world, so we could all get on with our lives. As the boys were doing so well, we knew we would soon be allowed to bring them home, which was both exciting and extremely daunting.

A few days after Christmas Minister Martin came to see us and to meet our precious twins. He was deeply moved by them and amazed at how wonderful they looked. He and his wife Mary gave them a musical mobile to hang on their cot, which helped bring some cheer to the clinical hospital environment. It felt very special to share our boys with him at last.

The next day the twins' occupational therapist, Kannan Natchimukhu, began helping us to try to find a suitable car seat for the boys; this was frustrating at times as there are no car seats designed for conjoined twins. He brought in several different types to see if any of them would suit. Sometimes trying to fit the boys into them would make us laugh; sometimes it just upset us that even this tiny thing was proving a major obstacle. Some days I felt really positive, but naturally I had my bad days when I felt heartbroken and overwhelmed by what my boys still faced. Whichever way I tried to look at it, there was no getting away from the fact that they were joined; they shared so much and we had no idea what the outcome would be, whether they would be suitable for separation when the time came, whether they would survive it, or be bound together for a short life. The nursing staff in Cork were a tower of strength, helping us to believe that it would all work out, and that anything was possible. They had grown quite close to the boys and would sometimes playfully argue over who would get to look after them as they all grew more confident in their care. I know their job is among the most difficult you can do: watching all those sick children, not knowing if they are going to pull through or not. Some of them really allowed themselves to grow close to our boys during the month they spent in the hospital, as they were doing well. It was such a feelgood situation. Many of these people are still in touch with me to this day and I cherish their friendship.

So, once again we were asked to come and meet with a medical team to put a plan together to bring our boys home. On the day in question my GP, Dr Lynda O'Callaghan, attended along with public health nurses, managers at CUMH, obstetricians and occupational therapists. I remember walking into the room to find Azzedine sitting there already. I literally had not seen him for longer than a few minutes in weeks. As soon as I came home from the hospital to the girls, he would leave to be with the boys. I sat down in the room with the medical team and I leaned over him and planted a kiss on his cheek and said, 'It's very nice to see you!' which caused everyone to giggle.

Slowly, a plan was formulated for bringing the babies back to Carrigtwohill. This time felt very different, however, as they were coming home with us: no more hospitals, no more nursing staff, just us. What saddened me a little was that when any new baby comes home there are usually balloons and relatives and cards and congratulations, but the boys were coming amid such secrecy I knew there would be nothing like this. I kept thinking about how we were going to be able to sneak them in and out of the house, or do normal things like grocery shopping. 'What am I going to tell people?' I wondered. 'What are Malika's friends going to ask her?' All these questions whirled around in my head and made me feel extremely uneasy.

One afternoon when I was cleaning up the house I came across a lovely hardcover notebook that I had got a few months previously. I had been keeping my own diary of my experiences, so I decided that it would be nice to turn that into a book of messages for the boys. Many people had said many moving things to me about my twins since their birth and I really wanted to record them so the boys could read them when they grew up. I knew I had a very difficult time ahead of me with their forthcoming separation surgery, the thought of which made it hard to breathe. I just had this idea that if I got people to write something down about the twins, I would be able to re-read all those lovely, positive empowering messages and draw strength from them during that impossible day. I also imagined showing them to the boys as adults so they might be able to grasp how they touched many people's hearts along the way. I got all the staff at the neo-natal ward to leave messages and later on I had gathered messages from people from all walks of life. There was even one from the President of Ireland, Mary McAleese. I treasure that book; I will always cherish it. People often found it difficult to say something to me about the twins, but I think they found it easier to write it down. Some of those messages were so touching and heartfelt that to this day they never fail to move me to tears.

One evening when Azzedine and I were in the family room of the hospital, we confessed to each other and admitted that we had been longing to stop hiding and to introduce our amazing boys to the world for quite some time. We desperately wanted to stop running. We felt our boys had fought so hard for life that they deserved a lot more than being hidden away. Why should we hide this wonderful gift we had been given? I called Micheál Martin to seek his advice. He suggested we talk to a man in Cork called Robin O'Sullivan who had a wealth of experience in public relations and knew how to deal with the media.

A meeting was set up between us and Robin, which was also to be attended by members of the Health Service Executive (HSE) South communications team to discuss how we were going to go about releasing information about our Little Fighters. We also had to contact GOSH to let them know that we were going to come out in public. The head of communications there jotted down a statement for us to take a look at, but I felt it was just too impersonal for our boys. I wanted the world to know how proud we were of them, and I decided to write a few lines myself. We wanted people to keep them in their thoughts. We were supposed to have a meeting about the media release in one of the conference rooms in the hospital, but I thought we should do it in the twins' room, so that day everyone came in to have a chat as I cared for the boys. This was the first time that Robin O'Sullivan met Hassan and Hussein and he thought they were beautiful. He was probably a little worried about how they would look at first, but it's like anything: it is scary until you know it and then you see it for what it is. I knew these boys were facing potentially life-threatening surgery, and I wanted the statement to be dignified but personal.

Finally, it was decided what to release and it was set to go out the very next day. I felt relieved, but also quite frightened. I knew there was no going back now. The statement I wrote said:

We are issuing a statement now because we feel the time is right to announce the twins' birth. We are very proud of our two little boys, and we feel blessed by their arrival six weeks ago. Presently, they are feeding well and gaining weight. We are planning for the boys to come home soon, and we are asking the media and the public to let us enjoy this special time with our 'two Little Fighters' before their separation later this year. We would also like to thank our family and friends who have helped us through such a difficult time and let them know just how much we appreciate their ongoing support.

It was brief and to the point, but had a personal touch. We thought it would go out that morning in the early news but there was some issue with the sign-off so it was not until 10.50 a.m. that it was released, in time for the 11 a.m. news. I remember vividly driving my car to the hospital when I heard it come out over the airwaves as part of the news bulletin of our local radio station, 96fm. As the newsreader read it out I had to pull over as my hands were shaking so much I thought I might crash the car. It was such a strange feeling to hear someone talking about your babies on the radio. I recall hearing the words: 'A pair of conjoined twins have been born to Cork parents' at which I found myself shouting at the radio, 'Those are my babies. Those are my boys!' tears rolling down my face. I ran to the twins' room and held them close. I prayed that I had done the right thing. I felt the walls closing in on us; I was nervous about how the media would portray them.

The very next day I got up at first light and headed to our local newsagent. I was greeted by such a bizarre sight! Every single newspaper on the shelf had the boys' story on the front page! I was happy to see that all the papers, from the tabloids to the broadsheets, had handled the story very sensitively. The message was carried in a very positive and dignified way. Many of the papers had picked up on the fact that I called the twins my 'Little Fighters' and this made me really happy. Nothing, however, could have prepared us for the subsequent reaction from the media. It was as if a whirlwind had picked up my little family and flung us into orbit. I remember the HSE communications manager, Angie O'Brien, coming to see me later that day with a thick folder full of media requests—everyone wanted more information. They wanted to know who we were; where the babies were joined; where we were from—all manner of information—each of them vying for that all-exclusive first interview. I immediately discounted the more clinical requests asking for information about their shared organs, etc. and kept the more personal ones, where journalists passed on their congratulations first and then politely asked to meet us, for consideration. There were requests from newspapers, TV stations and magazines. At first this completely overwhelmed me. I remember feeling quite paranoid and claustrophobic and pulling the blinds down in the boys' room as the media began to gather outside the hospital.

| MEETING THE PRESS

By the second week of January the full glare of the media spotlight had turned on us. There was nowhere left to run. The only thing standing between us and the frenzy outside was our advisor, Robin O'Sullivan. From the very first time I met him, I trusted him implicitly. He never once let me down, not for a moment. I used to affectionately call him 'my security blanket'. Every day Robin was dealing with hundreds of media requests; the appetite for news on the twins seemed insatiable. The poor man was supposed to be in retirement and had taken us on pro bono. I don't think I could ever truly express how grateful I am to him for everything he did for us. He was there every step of the way, a true gentleman. I consider him a great friend.

As each day went by more journalists tried to contact us from all over the country—they were even flying in from the UK! I was absolutely shocked when offers of money began to pour in for our story. Obviously, with Azzedine out of work, we were really beginning to feel the pinch, so any offer of money were initially tempting, but the idea of introducing the boys to the world for the very first time by selling their story to a newspaper just did not sit right with me. In those first few days after coming out publicly,

Robin received countless bids for our story. I remember him calling me one day to tell us that the media had begun a bidding war. This basically meant different tabloids were bidding against each other trying to get an exclusive story and the first photographs of us and the twins. They were offering obscene amounts of money for exclusivity. While all of this was going on over our heads the bank statements and bills kept piling in through the letterbox. I was afraid even to open them. I would just shove them in a drawer in the kitchen unopened. We had not paid our mortgage since before November and money was getting tighter and tighter. It had been a very lean Christmas, and an even leaner New Year.

The inescapable truth was if I took the money, then I would be better able to provide for my children, but nevertheless the thought of it made me feel queasy. I was frightened that by accepting a large amount of money for the boys' story we would be automatically forfeiting any control over how they would be presented to the world. I agonised over how they might want to focus on what was different about the twins, rather than what was special. I broke out in a cold sweat every time I thought about the possibility that they might want to take photos of my boys without their babygrows or to show how they were joined. This was to be the first time we would introduce our precious boys who had fought so bravely for life. I just couldn't accept money for that. I wanted them to be presented in a dignified and beautiful way as that was exactly how they were. I wanted to share this wonderful gift with the world, not sell it.

Azzedine and I spent hours discussing it and we agreed that we should turn down the offers and instead introduce the boys to the world freely through a medium of our own choosing. Coincidentally, the very day we turned down the substantial cash offers a bank statement came through the door informing us that we were not only penniless, but €500 in debt. As much as it frightened me to read this, I knew we had done the right thing; we may have been poor, but we were morally rich. We wanted the best possible start for the twins and we were convinced that selling their story was not it. Although things were a struggle we always concentrated on the bigger picture and that was that the boys were alive; they were here with us. Everything else, even penury, paled into insignificance in comparison with that. We were going to do it our own way and we were going to be in control of how it would happen.

We hired a local photographer named Daragh McSweeney from an agency in Cork called Provision, which Robin had recommended. We also decided to do a very short TV interview. Robin felt this would be the easiest way to introduce the twins without having to do an extensive interview. I was nervous at the prospect of appearing on television—every time I thought about it I would get a knot in my stomach, but we had agreed to do it, so I just had to swallow my fear. Robin invited two reporters, Paschal Sheehy from RTÉ and Paul Byrne from TV3, and told them we wanted to just introduce the boys and keep the interview very brief. On 18 January 2010, the reporters and their camera crews came up to CUMH to meet us. This was also the day the twins were being discharged and allowed to come home with us for the first time. I was excited about bringing my babies home, but equally I felt sick with nerves about the interview. Robin had warned us that the report and our family image could be picked up by news organisations, not just in Ireland, but all over the world, which seemed extraordinary.

I dressed hastily that morning, desperate to get to the hospital to see our gorgeous pair. I was trying to organise balloons and a welcome home banner for them as I really wanted it to be a special homecoming. Up until that point we had been unable to properly celebrate the fact that the twins were home in Cork because everything was shrouded in secrecy. I remember saying to the nurses that it might have taken six weeks, but I was going to fill their nursery with laughter and happiness and celebration.

I spent the morning agonising over how I should dress the twins for the interview. In the end, I decided on a dark blue babygrow for Hassan and a red and white one for Hussein: true Cork colours!

As we prepared for the camera crew's arrival we were shown into a light-filled room where the filming was to take place. The photographer came in first to take the photos. He was a lovely guy and told us he was happy just to be part of such a special day. He also allowed me to see the pictures he had taken to see if we were satisfied with them. We knew the following day was potentially going to be extremely intense, so it was in the back of our minds that our little family was soon going to lose its anonymity and this, of course, worried us. Throughout the photo shoot I could see the camera crew and the reporters, Paschal Sheehy and Paul Byrne, waiting outside to meet us. We could hear them speaking with Robin and every now and then I could see the top of a boom microphone or a camera and my stomach would tighten even more. Azzedine and I were so nervous at the thought of what was coming. After all, we were a normal family who had kept a pretty low profile up to this point, and now there was media outside our door ready to project our lives into thousands of homes all over the country.

Robin had briefed the reporters on how it was going to go before they were brought in and introduced to us. They were both extremely sensitive and overwhelmed to meet the boys and it wasn't long before the filming started. One of them asked me what I wanted to tell the world, so I just spoke from the heart. Throughout the interview I could see Iman off to my left pulling on and off my glasses and I thought I would just burst out laughing with nerves. After 10 minutes Robin stopped the interview and said that was enough for us. Afterwards we felt really proud that we had got through it, but equally relieved that it was all over! The cameramen packed up their equipment while we went down to collect the rest of the boys' things. We said our goodbyes to the lovely staff at CUMH and got ready to set out on our own: the six of us, at last. Ford Ireland gave us the use of a seven-seater van so we could travel home that day, and we were escorted from the hospital by their security in case there were any media lurking about. We'd finally managed to get a suitable car seat that the boys fitted snugly into, but they were already filling it, so we knew we weren't going to get a lot of time out of it. Off we headed towards Carrigtwohill in the snow and ice, laughing and singing and clapping along with baby songs. We were all so excited that we were finally bringing the boys home and could wash that hospital smell out of our clothes—at least for a while.

When the van finally came to a stop outside the house, I was overcome with emotion. I walked up the path with my brown-eyed sons under my arm and turned the key in the lock. I vividly remembered how badly I had felt the time I had locked that door before departing to London for the birth, the babies big in my belly, the agony of uncertainty, the lonely fear that dogged my every step. It felt like the bleakest, harshest never-ending mountain of which I would never reach the summit. I hardly dared to dream that I would be walking back through that door with both of those babies in my arms. I opened the door and whispered to them, 'You're home, boys, at last!' It was one of the finest moments of my life.

I showed them every room in the house that day, even our frosty back garden, while tears of joy streamed down my face. Malika had drawn some pictures for them, which we put up on the walls along with some balloons and a big banner. Later that evening we all sat down to watch the report on the 6 p.m. news. The girls were excited. It felt very strange to see ourselves on television, but we were proud of how it came across. The girls at Malika's school were so excited for her, they were even asking for her autograph, and I was delighted that she was getting a bit of attention for a change.

The following morning I took Malika to school and some of the other Mums walked right up to me, shook my hand and congratulated me. Some of them hugged me. It felt good not to have to hide any more, to be able to walk around with my head held high, breathing in the fresh air. It was as if I had been released from a dank underground cave and had just felt the sunlight on my face after so many lonely months in the darkness. That terrible secret evaporated there and then into the ether. It felt good to hear people compliment the twins and to see them being happy for me instead of those looks of pity and despair and those lowered eyes I had grown accustomed to.

The photograph was released to the media that day so my friend Joan called to take me to the local shop to see if the boys were in the papers. There was our little family staring back at us from every single newspaper on the shelf. We bought one of each that day to keep as mementoes. On the front of the *Star* there was a picture of myself, Azzedine and our boys and the headline read: 'Our Gift', which was my favourite headline. Every paper ran with a lovely positive story about us. I'm sure at that point it all started to make sense to people who knew us in our locality. Some of them must have been wondering why I had changed so much and become reclusive and depressed. Even the girls in our local shop must have noticed how I went from being a normal, happy customer to this shell of a woman, dressed in black, monosyllabic and broken. The majority of people who knew us were aware that I was having twins who had complications, but that was it. Now that the boys were home, I returned to my normal bubbly self.

As difficult as those first days were, I loved having the twins at home. The boys, however, would not settle at all; they cried all night—every night. We had put them in a cot in our bedroom. They had grown accustomed to the noise and lights of hospital wards and now suddenly they were lying in what must have seemed like an unearthly silence. There was no beeping of machines, or nurses coming in and out during the night. They were in a different cot in a pitch-dark bedroom; the poor things were not used to a normal home environment. It was amazing to have them home with us despite the sleep deprivation. I could hardly think straight from exhaustion. If one twin woke, the other would obviously wake too as they would scream and pull and tug and kick out at one another. Sometimes they would get frustrated with the proximity of the other and try to pull away. It was hard when they got frustrated because they were so close together; it tore me apart to watch. When they were crying, Hussein would often smack Hassan and this used to upset poor little Hassan. It wasn't all sorrow, though, a lot of the time they were comical to watch, and when they were asleep they were very peaceful with their little faces snuggled together and their arms wrapped around one another in innocent dreams.

By the third night we were absolutely dead on our feet. I remember Azzedine and I sitting up at around 3 a.m., holding two bottles, one in each little mouth. We were so tired we were literally holding each other up. At one point we looked at each other and just started to howl with laughter. I think perhaps the exhaustion rendered us half mad; that, coupled with the stress of the previous months, added to the absolute joy of having them home, just manifested itself in a laughing fit. We were laughing and crying at the same time, we were so happy. If it had been a normal pregnancy and the baby had kept us up for three nights straight we would have been stressed and cranky, but the joy of being kept awake by these two babies whom we thought we would never hear cry was immeasurable—their cries were like music to our ears.

One morning I came downstairs to find a letter had arrived from the hospital in Cork. I opened it to discover it was a notice of the twins' next appointment. I burst out laughing when I saw it as it said that Hassan was to be seen at 2 p.m. and Hussein at 2.30 p.m.! I thought about calling the hospital for a joke and saying Hassan couldn't make it, but I resisted the temptation! Another time when the boys were still conjoined the receptionist at the hospital asked me, 'Are they both going in?' to which I replied, 'Unless you have a better idea!' These were funny situations that made us laugh in the most difficult of times and I feel it was humour that got us through a lot of tough days.

That same morning our landline rang and when I picked it up it was the late Gerry Ryan's researcher asking if I would go on air. I was totally shocked that they had got my number and at first I was quite hesitant to go on, but in the end they convinced me. We chatted for a while about the boys and I told him that we had been having difficulties finding a suitable buggy and car seat for them as all the ones that were made for twins had a divide in the middle, which obviously was not suitable for our sons. Gerry kindly put out an appeal that day to anyone who might be able to help us, but nothing came of it. A few weeks later there was a knock on our front door and when I opened it, it was a lady called Angela Roche, the owner of a baby store in Dublin called Babybiz. I looked behind her and saw this amazing double pram called the Mountain Buggy, which was just right for the boys' needs. I stood looking at her in disbelief as she told me she had imported it all the way from New Zealand, it was worth in the region of €1,100 and she was just going to hand it over to us. I became very tearful. This total stranger had done all this for us! That pram was perfect; there was no way we could have gone anywhere as a family without it.

——

As time went on the media requests from newspapers and magazines kept pouring in. We knew it would probably be a good idea to do a more in-depth interview with a newspaper to take some of the media heat off, so after some consideration and advice from Robin we decided to go with the *Irish Examiner*. It was a national paper, but with a Cork connection and we had wanted to keep it as local as possible. We felt a bit nervous about our first proper interview as it is one thing releasing a statement to the media, but quite another to sit down and tell someone our story and allow people into our lives. On the day in question a Cork journalist with the *Irish Examiner,* Eoin English, and a lovely photographer, Denis Minihane, came down to meet us at home. I could tell they were both quite nervous when I answered the door, but I think as soon as they met the boys they loved them. They were extremely sensitive to our needs and we actually enjoyed the process a lot. I think they realised at once how calm and happy the house was despite our difficulties. We sat in the kitchen and talked through the whole story; they both held the boys and I think they understood how difficult it was for us. The next day they ran the story in the paper and we loved it. It was the dignified introduction to the world that our boys deserved.

Some days before this story appeared in the *Irish Examiner* Robin had received a request for us to go on 'The Late Late Show' with Ryan Tubridy. I was delighted with that request as I knew they would handle our story sensitively and we would get a chance to talk about our boys ourselves and present them in our own words. I knew that seeing us and the boys and how normal they were, despite being conjoined, would be totally different from reading about it. I felt people would really understand them better if they saw them. So when the invite came in we discussed it and came to the decision that no matter how well a newspaper article was written, or no matter how nice the pictures were, nothing could compare with being able to tell your own story yourself. We wanted people to know that we were two ordinary parents and these were two beautiful babies that just happened to be conjoined. RTÉ offered to fly us up, but we didn't want to risk the boys picking up an infection on a commercial flight, so we drove up in the seven-seater. We invited my Aunt Val to come along with us to give her a treat as she had done so much for us; I wanted to get a chance to thank her publicly. At this stage the boys were far too big for the car seat so I had to bring them on my lap.

During the drive up my phone rang. When I answered it, to my amazement it was someone from Áras an Uachtaráin asking us if we would like to call to meet the President of Ireland, Mary McAleese, and her husband for afternoon tea. I almost dropped the phone. I could not believe this—us meeting the President! I agreed and they told us a car would be sent to the Westbury Hotel, where we were staying that afternoon. Azzedine got a little stressed that we wouldn't have time to make it there and back before 'The Late Late Show', and he actually suggested we ask the President to reschedule for the next day! I said, 'Azzedine, this is the President of Ireland. You can't ask her to reschedule!' He quickly came to his senses and realised what he was suggesting and we all burst out laughing.

When we arrived at the elegant Westbury Hotel in Dublin and got out of the car, people immediately recognised us from the newspaper articles that had been written. As we were getting the boys out of the car lots of people came over and congratulated us and asked to see them. People were warm and positive towards us; they wanted to kiss the boys and stroke their cheeks. It felt so nice not to have to hide them and to be told how beautiful and special they were. The hotel manager, Joseph Downing, came out to meet us at the door. He was such a kind man, he couldn't do enough for us. A fellow Corkman, he showed us to our rooms, which were luxurious. There were strawberries and chocolates and lovely things laid out for us. It was such an indulgence after months in cramped accommodation and hospital beds. Soon a driver arrived to take us to Áras an Uachtaráin. He was so thrilled to meet us, he even phoned his wife on loudspeaker while we were in the car to tell her he had the 'famous' Benhaffaf twins in the car! It felt strange that this ordinary man was so excited about our babies. I talked to his wife over the phone and she even invited us to her house for tea! It was lovely to think that these total strangers had taken our boys to their hearts.

We eventually pulled in at the Áras and President McAleese's advisors came out to the front steps to greet us. I pleaded with Iman and Malika not to touch anything in the house! We were trying to bribe them with promises of rewards and sweets if they were good as we were led in to meet the President and Dr McAleese. I had butterflies in my stomach as I waited for them but I needn't have worried as they really were the most natural, lovely people. They played with the kids and just chatted with us. It was a wonderful, relaxed visit.

The girls were thankfully very well behaved. It was peculiar to think that just two months prior to this we were heading to London with an awful fear that our boys would not make it and now we were sitting in the President's house having afternoon tea. All the staff came in to hold the boys. There was nothing formal or staged about the whole experience; it just felt very natural. I was quite moved when the President told me she believed the way we had chosen to come out publicly had been very dignified. She also told me she believed my boys had brought the nation together, which filled me with pride. We had some photos taken with her and I asked her to put a message in the boys' book before we said our goodbyes. The minute they walked out of the room the girls started to go mad—they were playing the piano and going nuts! I was so relieved they had at least been well behaved when the President was in the room! Our driver arrived back for us again and it was off to the Westbury to prepare for the 'Late Late Show' appearance.

Between everything that needed to be done to get the children ready I had only a quick few minutes to dress myself for the show, which was a bit stressful! We were collected by another driver who drove us over to the RTÉ studios. As we were nearing Montrose I listened with dread as he told us that there was a large group of photographers waiting for us outside the studios. I pulled the babies close to me and felt anxious about what lay ahead.

Chapter 10 ～

| A COMMUNITY UNITES

The car finally came to a stop outside the studios and I caught a glimpse of the mob of photographers. I felt scared when I saw them, and was worried about the babies. At first I didn't want to get out of the car at all. I presumed that the moment we stepped out they would be in our faces, shouting and blinding us with flashes, doing everything they could to get a clear shot of the boys, but I couldn't have been more wrong. The driver opened the car door to help us out and we were greeted by a hushed silence. Slowly we began to walk forward and surprisingly nobody snapped us. I was waiting for this frenzy to start, but not one of them even raised a camera as we walked down the path. After a few moments one of the photographers said quietly, 'Would you mind if I took a picture of you and the babies?' He had asked so kindly that I said, 'Of course not,' and so he began to take some shots of us, as did the other photographers. Nobody stuck a camera in the boys' faces and not one of them took a shot without asking our permission first. Instead of the nightmare I had expected it to be, it was quite a positive experience. When it was over I was happy to leave the cold night air behind and be greeted by the warmth of the RTÉ studio.

Once inside we were shown to the Green Room where all the other guests were mingling, waiting to go on. Ryan Tubridy came in briefly to meet us—he was wonderful with the girls. They were a bit shy at first to meet him, but he soon got down on his knees to play with them and was teasing them and making them laugh and they loved him. It wasn't too long before it was our turn to go on. We had timed a bottle feed for just a few minutes before we were due to be called so the boys would be quiet and content for the interview. I remember standing behind a curtain and someone calling our name, so we handed the babies to Val and started to walk down those famous steps. I held on to Azzedine's arm for support and we walked on together. We were both unbelievably nervous. I tried to calm Azzedine down before we left the hotel by telling him to just imagine we were talking to someone we knew in their sitting room. I told him to try to avoid looking at the audience and the cameras, but it was nerve-racking. We were aware 'The Late Late Show' attracted a huge number of viewers so lots of people we knew would be watching.

Although it was a lovely, relaxed interview and we really got a chance to tell our story in our own words, it was also difficult because it was our first time speaking in public about the experience and having to go back through that emotional story, parts of which saw me break down in tears. The memory was like a fresh wound in my mind. Ryan was a consummate professional. When he saw I was upset, he would move on to Azzedine and vice versa. At one stage I looked at the audience and noticed some of them in tears as they listened to us. I wanted to lighten the mood somewhat and show that there was also such happiness when it came to our children. So when Ryan asked me what the future held for Hassan and Hussein, instead of giving him a serious response I told him that my pair would 'give Jedward a run for their money', at which the audience laughed and clapped. Ryan invited the girls on to join us and Val brought the boys out. Ryan asked if he could hold our little bundle. Later he told me it was a precious moment and he would never forget feeling their tiny hearts beating next to his own.

I was relieved when it was done and dusted and we were shown back to the Green Room for a breather. I was aware that Heather Mills was another guest on the show that night, so I asked if I would be allowed to speak with her privately. At this stage I had not told anyone that the boys had only one leg each. I used to keep them wrapped up in a blanket so nobody would see. I just didn't feel ready to share that awful truth with the world, but here was a woman who was the role model for amputees. I was not going to miss out on an opportunity to speak with her! She was most helpful and inspirational. She gave me her email address and mobile number and said she would love to come to see the boys again. She asked me to call her if the separation was a success. She is still in contact with us to this day. I felt that her being on 'The Late Late Show' that night was one of a series of coincidences that helped me to believe that everything would turn out well for my boys in the end.

After the show we went back to the Westbury Hotel. I was very touched by the fact that the manager, Joseph, had waited for us to return and even brought some homemade cookies and milk to our room for the girls. We were so pampered, we didn't want to go home! The next morning we checked out and Joseph gave me a huge hug. He wished us all the best. I thanked him for being so kind to us and for making us feel important. He said, 'But you are important!' as we closed the car door and set off for home.

Following the 'Late Late' appearance there was a barrage of calls from the media looking for interviews and photographs. I believe that it was from that point on the boys really captured the hearts of the nation. I think perhaps they understood a bit more what we were going through. Some of the media attention was completely bizarre, however. One day I got a call from a journalist working with a tabloid newspaper asking me if my boys were going for their vaccinations and could I make a comment. I asked this individual if either of my two little girls were getting routine vaccinations, would they be doing a story on it; he said no, so I said, 'Then why do you think I would feel comfortable with you doing something on my boys and sensationalising this most routine of things?' Sometimes I became so exhausted and worried that the media attention really wore me down. After all, I knew what the boys were still facing. It was like a cancer in my bones— every day it haunted me.

Azzedine and I had made a decision not to reveal too much about how many organs the boys shared and how complicated it was going to be to separate them, as we thought it was a private family matter, just like the fact that they had only two legs. We wanted to respect their privacy as they didn't have a voice of their own, and it was our job to protect them. Quite often the media would report that they didn't share any organs, which used to upset me, but I knew it was best we kept it quiet for now. Knowing ourselves was burden enough without putting that terrifying truth out there for everyone around us to take in. I honestly thought people would find it upsetting if they knew just how much they shared and what would have to be separated.

A few days after we returned to Cork we agreed to do an at-home interview with our local paper, the *Evening Echo*, which is a Cork institution. I was delighted with the way our family was portrayed in that first piece in the *Echo*. The local paper continues to be very supportive of us today. They really took our plight to their hearts and there were some absolutely beautiful pieces about the boys over the following months. The articles always focused on the positives and what a lovely, happy atmosphere there was in our home for our children and I loved that. Letters of support from total strangers began to pour in to the *Evening Echo* offices, which the editor would print regularly. Some of these were so touching that they moved me to tears. It was when I read those heartfelt and moving letters I began to understand just what kind of support was out there for us and our boys and it helped me find the strength to start going out as a family. I remember the first time that we went out, all six of us, to the local grocery store. I was quite nervous about it as I knew that people would recognise us, but once again I was totally taken aback by the kindness of strangers. Every second shopper stopped to hug us and congratulate us. I was overwhelmed by how respectful people were. Nobody came over just for a look at the twins, but instead they embraced us and shared stories with us about their own children and difficulties in their own lives. It was nice to do something as a normal family; something so run of the mill as buying groceries had seemed impossible just a few weeks previously.

When requests began to pour in from documentary makers who wanted to make a film about the boys, I gave the idea serious consideration. When I was pregnant with the twins I had watched lots of documentaries on conjoined twins, which helped me to understand what was happening to me. I thought it important that I make a film, so other women, who might find themselves desolate, alone and pregnant, could find some support in watching how our family coped. It was of huge importance to me, however, that we picked the right people for the job and a crew that wanted to make a documentary the same way we did: the human story of conjoined twins. I didn't want anything that was fundamentally focused on the medical side of things. There were eight different groups vying to make the film at one time, but in the end we decided to go with ITN as their pitch had appealed to me the most. They had said they were interested in portraying us as a family and showing the world how the boys had changed our lives. I wanted to make a moving documentary. I wanted people to realise just how special and beautiful conjoined twins were. For me it was my duty and my mission to try to help change the world's perception of these twins. I felt I owed it to my boys.

We were told a film crew would come from London to meet us within a matter of days. I had a good feeling about the team from the start and I was right. I set down a couple of ground rules such as under no circumstances were my boys to be filmed naked, which the crew agreed to. I also explained to them that we wanted this to be a documentary that would tell our story and show the world how amazingly gorgeous the boys were, and how despite their complications they were two healthy babies and we were going to do everything in our power to give them the best life they could possibly wish for. What sealed the deal for me was the fact that one of the female producers who had flown over to meet us had a prosthetic limb. I remember at the time feeling that fate was, once again, intervening for my boys.

It wasn't long before a fund-raising drive for the boys' started to kick off in our local community, for which I will be forever grateful. People understood that with Azzedine out of work—and the financial burden we faced during what was going to be an indefinite stay in London for the twins' separation surgery—we needed help. There were coffee mornings and quiz nights and all sorts of imaginative things held to raise money. It was overwhelming that so many people came together to help Hassan and Hussein and the outpouring of love that came from that very first coffee morning, which was organised by some local Mums, was beyond words. I had never experienced anything like it. At this point the twins were eight weeks old and people knew they had to undergo separation surgery at some stage, but nobody knew just how soon it would be.

One afternoon my brother Jason called to the house to tell us that John McCarthy of the Rebel Riders Motorcycle Club in East Cork had approached him to ask if I would be happy to allow them to organise a bike run in aid of our boys. The run was going to go from Midleton to Dungarvan. I cried in my kitchen at the thought of somebody being so generous and kind. The event quickly gathered momentum and a launch was organised for Saturday, 13 February at the Lee Motorcycles Club in Little Island. I was totally overwhelmed by the numbers that turned out that day. I remember being asked to say a few words and choking back tears as I spoke. I found it amazing that all these strangers would come together to help us. There were hundreds of big strong bikers standing shoulder to shoulder for our two tiny babies. The sight of that sea of people was incredible. I noticed some of the men were in tears after we spoke about the boys, which was deeply moving. Without the support of those fundraisers we couldn't have kept going at that time and I don't think I could ever thank all those amazing people enough. This, along with the steady flow of letters and cards from the public, was what got us through such a dark and uncertain time.

The morning of the bike run, 6 March, I got up early to dress the boys as warmly as possible as it was one of those bitterly cold but fantastically bright spring days. We knew the run had attracted a lot of interest, but nothing could have prepared us for the hundreds and hundreds of bikers and supporters who turned up that day at the Two Mile Inn in Midleton. I turned the corner to the Inn and saw these endless rows of bikes: shiny steel and leather. It just knocked our socks off. None of these people knew us and yet here they were in their hundreds. It warmed my heart to see these tough, leather-clad men and their monstrous motorbikes all out for our two tiny boys and their mammoth struggle for life.

Before the boys were born I had often thought how the world was such a cruel and heartless place. People could be so terrible to one another that I would often despair at having to bring up little children in such a dreadful place, but Hassan and Hussein's arrival changed my view of people utterly. I could see a new beauty in them, like a caterpillar that had grown breathtakingly beautiful wings. People from all walks of life came together for those boys: young, old, rich, poor—everyone from bikers to ministers, doctors to politicians stood shoulder to shoulder for them. More than 1,400 bikers took part: a mind-blowing number. Nothing could compare with the atmosphere that day. It was the biggest bike run Ireland had ever seen! I remember the deafening roar of all of those bikes revving up for our Little Fighters as they headed out on to the main road filling the air with exhaust fumes and hope. It was a phenomenal day; the country was in serious financial meltdown and yet all of these people were willing to give to our boys. I will never forget that day or those people. I hope they realise just how much they helped us and how we will be forever grateful to them all. Azzedine and I were having our own private celebration that day too as we were 13 years together, which was made all the more special by virtue of the fact that the boys were 13 weeks old!

The following Saturday, 13 March, was a very important day for us as it was the boys' Naming Ceremony, which is like a christening. I decided to hold the event at the Go Safari play centre in Carrigtwohill. We invited friends and family along and certain members of the media who had been supportive to us. As everyone would be together that day, I decided to take the opportunity to break the news about the boys' separation surgery, which was just over three weeks away. I dressed the twins up in cute cow-print babygrows. I knew we had to break this awful and distressing news to everyone, but I also knew that it was supposed to be a happy occasion, a nice memory for the girls. People were laughing at my chosen venue, but I wanted it to be all about the children that day and not the adults. We had a lovely private room for our party where we had laid out a gorgeous spread for the children. I remember all of these smiling faces, everyone there to celebrate with us.

I could barely hold back my tears from the moment I walked in. I just wanted to get the announcement out of the way so we could get on with celebrating this happy occasion in our sons' lives. Amid the blue-frosted cakes and the brightly coloured sweets I announced the shocking news to my guests. I thanked everyone for coming before telling them that we had been given a date for the boys' surgery: it was going to take place on 7 April at Great Ormond Street Hospital in London. People seemed genuinely shocked that we were going to have to leave Ireland within a week to prepare for their surgery. I found it quite difficult to get the words out at all, to release them into the air where they would become all the more real. I just couldn't stop crying as Azzedine squeezed my shoulder in support. The announcement went out on the 6 p.m. news bulletin later that evening. I asked people to keep the boys in their hearts and prayers.

The next day was Mother's Day. I remember the blissful happiness of waking up to find all four of my children around me, the fire on and the general hustle and bustle of a normal family day. I looked down at my bright-eyed boys and thanked God they were there with me. After opening the decorative and glitter-filled cards the girls had made for me I had this sudden realisation that my boys had never seen the sea. I decided to make that day particularly special in case it was the only Mother's Day I would ever share with my twins. The six of us filed into the van and drove down to Youghal beach on a sharp and crisp afternoon. As we stepped onto the sand, I told my crying boys to smell the sea air and to listen to the crashing waves. I told them if they survived their separation I would bring them back there so they could be free like the birds that flew over our heads. I looked out to sea and I prayed my boys would be back here with me in December for their first birthday, separated, laughing and free.

As part of the documentary process, Azzedine and I were interviewed by ITN *Tonight*'s Julie Etchingham. I found this very difficult, as we went through every single stage since we discovered the boys were conjoined through to their birth and its aftermath; it brought it all back to us and was an exhausting process. There were a few occasions where I broke down and we had to stop filming for a while, but she was a very sensitive person and I was delighted that Azzedine really opened up and talked about what the whole experience had felt like for him as a father. He spoke very eloquently and with great feeling and I was very proud of him.

However, every night I lay awake, thinking about what my boys were facing. I was so frightened I could hardly breathe.

Chapter 11 ∽

| RETURNING TO LONDON

Even though we were due to travel to London in a few short days we just could not face packing our bags. I absolutely dreaded dragging those suitcases out all over again, filling them with our fear and uncertainty. That last week before we left Cork was one of the most difficult we ever experienced—there were lots of tears and crying silently into pillows. On the one hand we were trying to get things organised for the journey, while on the other we just wanted to hold on to every precious moment we had with the twins at home. Sometimes I would look down on their sleeping heads and feel such a burning sense of guilt. I'd think about picking up my phone and calling the whole thing off, but I knew that would have been selfish. There was a lot of organisation involved prior to our departure. Minister Martin helped to arrange an Air Corps ambulance to bring us back to London. While the boys' team at CUMH was busy planning their handover, the team in London was preparing for their arrival. We didn't want to take our boys from their happy home and hand them over to cruel fate.

Poor Malika had to say goodbye to her friends all over again, which really upset her, and once again I felt dreadful about it. She would ask me, 'Mummy, are we going back to the other world to unstuck the boys?' which always made me smile. She was so innocent. It broke my heart to see her worry so much about them. When I looked at her and Iman at play I would feel suddenly panicked. All of these unthinkable scenarios would swirl around in my head. What if they didn't make it? What would I tell Malika and Iman? Would their childhood be ruined? It's a very difficult thing to try to explain to a child that their siblings are going to hospital for a big operation as you try to protect your child from fear and worry and yet you don't want to lie to them in case it all goes horribly wrong. Malika knew they were going to be separated and when she asked me how the doctors were going to do it I had to think on my feet. I remember her limpid pools of eyes filling with tears as she asked me whether they were going to cut them and hurt them. I told her that the doctors were going to use very special, bright, magic lights that would separate the boys and then they would sprinkle them with fairy dust to make them well. It was hard to keep it together for her while the truth screamed and roared relentlessly in my own head. I rubbed her brow and told her there was no need to worry, that the boys were not going to feel any pain. Thankfully, she believed this.

During that last week the documentary crew would often come in and out to film us, but by this stage I was locked in a world of fear, so I barely registered their presence. We knew we would have to say goodbye to everyone who had grown close to the boys, which I was not looking forward to. Finally, on the Friday before we were to set off, we took out the dreaded suitcases. Our flight was not due to depart until Sunday, 21 March, but we were leaving our home on the Saturday night in a bid to avoid media attention. We didn't know how long we would be away for or if we would be bringing our sons home with us—both of them, one of them or neither one. Doing that once was horrendous; having to do it again felt like absolute cruelty.

We had become so attached to the boys since their birth. They were my heart and soul, the very air I breathed. They were everything to us. As parents, you think: 'They are happy and healthy the way they are and at least we would have a certain number of years with them if we don't go ahead with the separation, whereas if we allow them to be separated and they don't make it we are cutting that time short.' It was an impossible decision, but we knew in our hearts it was better for them to be separated. Even though the temptation was there to leave them together, we had to think of the bigger picture: they needed separate lives. They needed to be free from one another in order to have the best chance at survival.

Their hearts were lying very close together and we knew that was not good. Throughout the pregnancy their hearts had always been strong, but a few weeks before their separation Mr Kiely told us that although they had been good since the birth, they weren't great, so we knew they were already starting to weaken. For me the decision to separate them finally came one day when he told me plainly, 'If we leave them together they will never stand, never walk. Life together would be a grim vista. They wouldn't have long.' When we weighed up all the options, we knew the best thing we could do for them was give them a real chance at life. It was the toughest decision we ever had to make, or ever will have to face. We did question it, though, constantly, right up to the moment we handed them over.

The kids said goodbye to their friends while our neighbours and close friends came to our house to say goodbye to the twins. That Saturday was one of the saddest I have ever lived through. All day long, friends, neighbours, and family members filed in and out of the house, with lowered eyes and bent heads. It felt like a wake: grown men, women, and children came through the door— all of them left in tears. They came to wish us luck and kiss the boys goodbye, not knowing if it was a last goodbye. Some people said they honestly did not know how they were supposed to say goodbye; others chose not to come at all because they found it an impossible thing to do.

I was sick with anxiety about what lay ahead; I couldn't believe it had come around so quickly and once again we were preparing to disappear in the night like fugitives. I was tired of worry, tired of planes, tired of hospitals and sick and tired of London. The horror of fearing for the lives of our children was like a slow sickness that lived in our blood, multiplying in our cells with every passing minute. It was one thing bonding with the babies when I was pregnant, but it was quite another having had them in my arms for months, watching their smiles and their ways. Their smell had nestled under my skin. To even think about having to hand over that precious cargo, which had been such a part of our lives for the previous four months, felt like being stabbed repeatedly in the heart.

All day long good luck cards arrived at the house from well wishers. The media coverage, what I saw of it flickering away on the TV, was very positive. The one thing I had asked of people was to keep the boys in their thoughts and their prayers and it felt so nice that in the weeks leading up to the separation every media organisation carried that same message. I know that many people prayed for those little boys and I owe them a great deal for that. It really was all of those people's prayers and positive thoughts that carried us through those difficult months.

So, finally we got ourselves together and said our goodbyes. Locking up the house was an impossible task: I burst into tears at the thought that the boys might not be with me the next time I opened the door. I remember thinking to myself: 'How many times can we do this?' We had done it for the birth. How could we have to do this again? The media was reporting that the boys didn't share any major organs, but we knew they shared much and were facing an extremely risky surgery where anything could go wrong. For the previous four months I had woken up thinking of it every morning and had gone to sleep dreaming of it every night. I was haunted by 'what ifs?' What if they don't make it? What if one of them dies? They were far too precious to lose. So many nights I had spent locked in our en suite bathroom wailing into a towel so the girls wouldn't hear me. Azzedine turned to his religion and his prayer: he accepted what God had in store for the boys. He used to say, 'God gave us these boys and we were happy. We must always be grateful for the time we had with them no matter what happens.' But I would say, 'These are my babies. How can I think about letting them go?' To let one child go under the knife was brutal; to risk losing two was a living hell.

We stayed at the airport hotel that last night in Cork to avoid the media. It was impossible to sleep—we were numbed by fear. We were trying to not let the girls see how anxious we were, but it was tough. I knew having the girls with us was the right thing to do, as we would have fallen to pieces without them. They gave us a purpose and a reason to keep tying those ever-fraying edges together. As minutes turned into hours that night I kept looking at my boys' perfect little heart shape and their peaceful sleeping heads. I got down on my knees and begged God to help us. Part of me believed that I had fought so hard for those babies that no God would take them from me. I deserved to keep them! The girls deserved them; they loved their little brothers completely. I don't think any sisters in this world could have loved their brothers more.

I tried to sleep that night, but I just couldn't help watching the boys sleep. I knew how much I was going to miss that sight of them joined together. They were my heart. When I imagined them being separated, it filled me with sadness. To divide them seemed cruel. They were happy, healthy boys always smiling and gurgling and feeding and keeping us up all night. I would often suffer what I can only describe as a panic attack when I would imagine what they would have to go through. How could I hand them over to those surgeons? How could I be expected to hand over my heart and soul? I really thought I wouldn't be able to do it when the time came. I remember making a solemn promise that night that I would make myself available to any other parents who might find themselves going through what we were going through. Nobody came to our aid—we had to go through it all on our own. Nobody understood—there was no support group for this. There was nothing but the frozen grasp of fear.

The doctors deliberately kept a lot of the detail of the operation from us, and probably with good reason. They would tell us what we needed to know and not give us any more information, but the one thing that played over and over in my mind was how they were going to separate my boys. I was imagining all sorts of terrifying scenarios and the idea of it would cut through my own grinding heart. I just about managed to deal with the idea of their organs being separated, but the thought of somebody cutting through my precious babies' bones almost ended me. It lived in my head constantly. Because I knew so little about how the internal organs worked, this part of the surgery didn't haunt my mind much, but anyone can imagine what it would be like for someone to saw through your bones: it was the stuff of horror films. Here I was looking at my sons and imagining how, in a matter of days, someone was going to cut my perfect babies in half. You look at them now and you would not harm a hair on their heads, but back then they were even tinier.

Morning finally came, as much as I willed it not to. We were informed by the hotel receptionist that Micheál Martin, a police escort and an ambulance crew were waiting for us downstairs, waiting to bring us right down on to the runway. Minister Martin came to see us off, which was a lovely gesture, and I was so glad to see a friendly face. By the time we came down to reception we were shaking with nerves. This was it. We had to leave and the next time we would touch down in Cork Airport we didn't know if we would have our two boys in our arms or in two tiny, white coffins. Minister Martin kissed the twins goodbye and wished us good luck. I broke down and told him how scared I was. He told me the Irish embassy in London would be in constant contact and he would be keeping in touch with them. He said our boys were in the best possible hands. He told me the surgeons were all very confident it would be a good outcome for the boys and they were in the hands of some of the best experts in the world, but it didn't make it any easier to get on that plane.

The flight on the way over was painfully quiet. Nobody spoke. I think the crew saw how devastated we looked and knew how precious that cargo was to us. The twins' nurse at CUMH, Anne Buckley, had met us at the airport to assist in the transportation. She looked forlorn during the flight. I think she became quite attached to the twins during their stay in CUMH and I could see when we arrived in Northolt that she was overcome with emotion as she said goodbye to us. None of us, not even the girls, spoke on the journey from Northolt to our new accommodation on Great Ormond Street. We went up to the flat and wearily set down our luggage.

We were supposed to admit the boys that very day, but I just couldn't let go. I was holding the boys and hugging them—I physically felt unable to part with them. Azzedine tried to coax them from me. He said, 'But, Angie, you will never be ready to part with them. There will never be a right time!' but I just refused. How could I? Eventually he rang the hospital and explained that I wasn't ready to hand them over, so they gave us until 7 a.m. the following morning. I didn't put them down once that night. I wanted to protect them and hold them and whisper to them that everything would be OK. Before long it was morning and while Azzedine and the girls slept, I got up at 6 a.m. to get the twins ready and to make the lonely journey over to the hospital. I was nervous that the media would be waiting for me below, but thankfully it was so early there was nobody about.

I brought the boys back to the Woodland Ward where they had been cared for before we went home. As hard as it was to return to that ward, I knew the staff and the boys' room well, so at least there was some familiarity there. I had to stand back while the nurses formally admitted them. I was in pieces—I couldn't hold it together at all. The nurses were wonderfully supportive. They were trying to be really positive and tell me everything was going to be OK, but I was frightened for my children. The first thing the boys had to undergo was a general anaesthetic and a CT scan. This was to be the start of a full week of tests that would culminate in a decision as to whether they could be separated.

I had to leave them while they went for the tests—it was very hard when I could hear their sorrowful cries. I remember asking one of the staff involved to them to give them a cuddle to soothe them. I went back to the apartment to help make breakfast for the girls. I needed to reassure them that the boys were OK and they would get to see them in the evening. An hour later I got a call from the hospital to say the twins were in the recovery area, so I could come back. When I arrived, Hassan was still asleep and Hussein was waking up. They were still very groggy. I badly wanted to pick them up so they would smell me and know I was there for them.

We didn't at any stage want to leave the boys alone. Even though they had nurses with them, they had had four months of being with Mum and Dad, so we swapped shifts to be with them at all times. I felt split in two myself trying to put on a happy face for the girls before going headlong into that maelstrom of worry with the boys, knowing what was ahead of them: the upset, the pain. On Tuesday the boys had an ultrasound examination to see if they had one or two gall bladders. The experts took lots of detailed scans in the hope of finding two, which would bode very well for the separation. They found only one. The next day the boys underwent a urology investigation, which they had a very bad reaction to. It became quite chaotic all of a sudden with monitors beeping and doctors and nurses running around looking very serious and concerned. I was petrified. I couldn't even speak. The cardiac expert was called as their heart rate began to soar. I started to think I was going to lose them. They did not look good at all—they were fire engine red and their heartbeats were very rapid, but mercifully this calmed down eventually and they went back to their lovely honey colour. There was more good news later that day when we learned that the hole in Hassan's heart had closed up. This seemed nothing short of a miracle to us. It was the first bit of really good news we had got for a while and for a moment it felt like I had stopped falling down an endless, dark shaft.

The staff at both UCLH and GOSH were extremely supportive through all of the tests and subsequent waits, and on days when Azzedine and I needed to visit the hospital together, our nurse friends from UCLH would come and take the girls to the park, or out for an ice cream. The number of cards and good wishes that poured into the hospital every day was incredible. Friends at home told me that people all over Cork had taped photographs of the boys to the inside of their front windows under which they had lit candles. Others were lighting candles in churches and their places of worship. When I heard this, I felt so moved.

The next raft of tests was on their kidneys, the results of which showed they each had one good kidney and one bad one, which they would lose. The pressure of these constant tests and subsequent agonising waits for results felt like a heavy wall that was slowly but surely bearing down on us. We thought the operation would be called off when the doctors discovered that on Hussein's side the liver had an input and an output of blood but they could see no such supply for Hassan, which would mean if they were separated he could well die. I thought I would pass out from worry. It was such an impossibly hard situation because even if they told us the separation could go ahead, we still faced losing both of them, but at that stage we had psyched ourselves up for it and if it were not to happen, it would have been unbearable. Following another raft of tests, they thankfully discovered that both boys had blood supplies going into and out of the liver. To say that was a weight off our minds is an understatement.

Finally, Saturday, 27 March came around and we were told we could take the boys back to our accommodation for a family week. When the girls woke up and found their little brothers were there, they were ecstatic. We had one week together—maybe our last—

and we were going to enjoy every second of it. One week left with our little heart-shaped twins joined together, the way we loved them. We took the boys to the park on a beautiful spring afternoon. The girls ran and played and swung higher and higher on the swings and waved to their brothers. It was lovely to be away from the hospital and to be together on those days despite the icy grip fear had around my heart. I could almost pretend that we were all at home enjoying a normal family day out and there was no hospital or surgeons or pain waiting for us less than a mile down the road.

The following day it was back to reality with a loud bang when we were summoned to a meeting with Mr Kiely at which he was to give us a summary of all the tests that had been done over the previous seven days and let us know once and for all whether the operation was still going ahead. He told us things were looking very positive, which was an enormous relief, but on Sunday, 4 April, three days before their surgery, the boys developed an infection. They were vomiting and had terrible diarrhoea and their temperatures went sky high to 39 degrees. They were terribly ill and I was so worried the operation wouldn't happen. I stayed at their bedside night and day just willing them to get better. It was touch and go, but once again their Little Fighters' spirit shone through and they recovered just in time.

On the Monday before their surgery we brought the boys to the park for the last time. I remember showing them the flowers and the trees and the bumble bees and the little squirrels and promising them when they were a little older they would run and play with their sisters and take turns on the swings and would never ever have to feel pain again.

———

A few days after we had returned to Cork in December, I was cleaning up the house when I came across a poem that I had started to write for the boys when we were in London. I had thought it had been lost, but when I discovered it I decided to put pen to paper again. I grabbed any spare moment to work on it and when it was completed, I was quite proud of how it turned out. I decided to send it to Robin. I felt quite shy showing him these words that had been pulled straight from the very channels of my heart, but I knew he would be honest with me. He told me I should release it to the media as it would help people to understand what I was going through and might remind them to pray for my boys. So, on the night before their separation, the poem was released with a statement attached asking people to keep the boys in their hearts. It said:

The family of Cork's conjoined twins has requested prayers and support as Hassan and Hussein Benhaffaf prepare for their separation procedure at Great Ormond Street Hospital in London tomorrow. 'We have been overwhelmed by the genuinely supportive response of so many people since the announcement of our Little Fighters' birth. Now as they face this critical operation we renew our appeal for everyone's thoughts and prayers, especially tomorrow morning, which will help sustain our boys and our whole family at this most important time.' For the past fortnight the boys and their family have been in London and have undergone tests in preparation for the surgery. In meetings with the surgical team under Mr Edward Kiely, the Cork-born expert in the separation of conjoined twins, they have been briefed on the thorough preparations which have been made. The boys will be brought into the hospital today having spent the weekend with parents Azzedine and Angie and their sisters Malika and Iman. Angie Benhaffaf has been keeping a written record of her innermost thoughts and feelings since it was shown in a scan during the earlier part of her pregnancy that she was carrying conjoined twins. She completed it at the end of last week. 'It's what really came out from my heart,' she says.

Here is the full text of the poem:

I loved you both from the very start, when doctors thought you shared one heart.

I cried so much during that time; we did not think that all would be fine.

Your two big sisters got me through the worst. I really felt that I had been cursed.

For eight months I was in such a lonely place as the birth was something I thought I couldn't face.

But then came that beautiful winter's morn, on the 2nd of December my 'little fighters' were born!

To hear you both cry was music to our ears.

Your dad and I cried so many tears.

You both have given me courage and strength, what a wonderful 'gift' we have been sent!

'Hassan' is the quiet one, and a minute older, 'Hussein' is the naughty one—he's a little bit bolder!!

Two wonderful boys joined together in love.

You truly are a 'gift' sent from above.

I feel so honoured to be your mum.

I need just one more miracle to come.

'The little fighters' is the name ye share.

You have earned it well, as you fought to be here.

Your final battle is getting near.

We are all behind you, so have no fear.

Boys—you have filled us all with love and hope, without you both, we would never cope.

Keep on fighting to stay strong, always remember your big sisters' song.

'You are not alone' is the song they sing for you, and those words could not be more true!

So as we prepare for the surgery ahead, Many a tear will be shed.

All I can ask of God now, is that ye feel no pain, I'm so proud of
my boys—'Hassan and Hussein'.
No matter how this will all end, I am forever grateful for the time
we did spend.
You have brought the country together, in love and prayer,
You have made 2010 a special year!
Always remember, 'You are not alone', Please God someday, we'll
all return home.
I feel I must be one of the luckiest mums, to have not one, but two
precious sons.
Love you both with all my heart and soul
Mummy xx

I remember all the newspapers ran with it and it was read by thousands of people on the RTÉ website. Messages flooded in from people at home who wanted to tell me that we were not alone—they were thinking of us and wishing us well and willing our boys to live. It was incredibly moving to receive all of these messages in our darkest hour. It meant so much that all these people would be praying for our little boys as they faced their biggest battle.

———

Finally the moment came when we had to admit our Little Fighters for their surgery. I slowly got the boys' hospital bag together. I could barely see through my tears. I put all their good luck cards and the message book and photos of them that had been taken at the bike run and with their sisters into the bag and shut the door behind me. This was it.

My family meeting with the President and Dr McAleese at Áras an Uachtaráin, 29 January 2010.

Me, Ryan Tubridy, Iman and the twins at 'The Late Late Show', 29 January 2010.

My favourite photo of the boys at home, February 2010. (*Irish Examiner*)

Me, Azzedine and the twins at home, February 2010. (*Irish Examiner*)

Hassan and Hussein with their loving big sister Iman (aged two and a half), February 2010. (*Irish Examiner*)

Multi-tasking! Azzedine and me feeding both twins at once at home, February 2010. (*Irish Examiner*)

The Little Fighters the night before their Biggest Battle, 6 April 2010. (© *Medical Illustrations Great Ormond Street Hospital NHS Trust*)

The night before the separation surgery with the twins' obstetrician from UCLH, London, Mr Pat O'Brien, 6 April 2010.

The night before the separation, with the twins' special message book, good luck cards and photos from the bike run and with their family, 6 April 2010.

The night before the separation with our precious boys. The last photo of them 'conjoined', 6 April 2010. (© *Medical Illustrations Great Ormond Street Hospital* NHS *Trust*)

Success! Happy faces as the twins survive their separation. Me, Azzedine and Malika outside GOSH, London, 8 April 2010. (© *Lee Durant/National Pictures*)

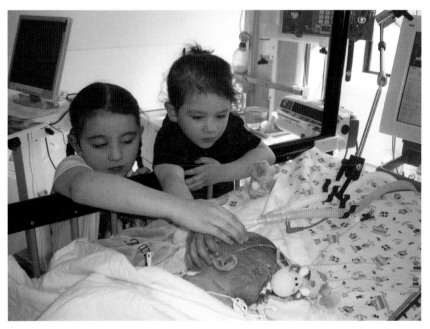

Malika and Iman see the boys separated for the first time, 24 April 2010, 17 days after their separation.

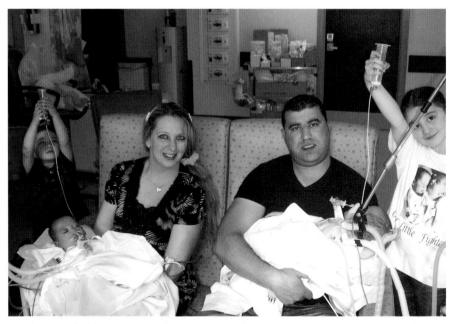

Our first time holding Hassan and Hussein since they were separated, as the girls feed them milk from feeding tubes, 25 April 2010.

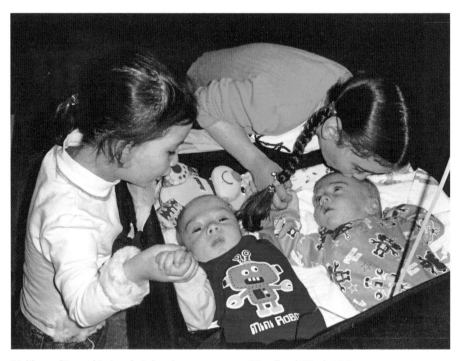

Malika and Iman kissing their brothers at GOSH on Woodland Ward, 8 May 2010.

Six weeks after separation! Hassan, Hussein and family with the gifted surgeons, Mr Edward Kiely and Prof Agostino Pierro, who separated them at GOSH, London; before they returned to Cork, 20 May 2010.

Happiness at last! The day all six of us returned to Cork with the Air Corps, here with Minister Micheál Martin, and Cork Airport staff. (*Daragh McSweeney/Provision*)

Azzedine and me with Hassan and Hussein after touching down in Cork Airport, 21 May 2010. (*Daragh McSweeney/Provision*)

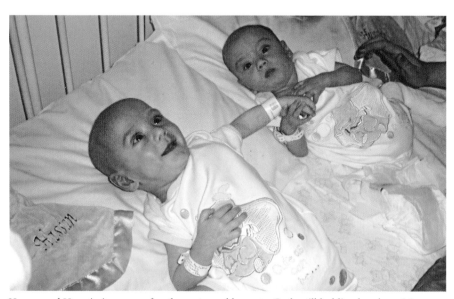

Hassan and Hussein in cumh after they returned home to Cork, still holding hands, 23 May 2010.

The Civic Reception held for the twins at Cork City Hall by the Lord Mayor and Lady Mayoress, Dara and Tanya Murphy, 16 June 2010. (*Niall Carson/PA Wire*)

Hassan and Hussein in the Cork GAA jerseys given to them by the Lord Mayor of Cork, Cllr Dara Murphy, 16 June 2010.

Azzedine and me, taken at the 'Miriam Meets' show, 19 June 2010.

Hassan and Hussein with their loving big sisters Malika and Iman, September 2010. (*Pixifoto Cork*)

Brotherly love! Hassan and Hussein all smiles, 29 August 2010.

The Maternity and Infant Awards, November 2010, at the Shelbourne Hotel, Dublin. The family received a Special Merit Award for Courage and Bravery in extremely difficult circumstances during Pregnancy, Birth and Separation. (*Ashville Media Group*)

Azzedine and I proudly holding our Little Fighters, Hassan and Hussein, at the Maternity and Infant Awards, November 2010. (*Ashville Media Group*)

A precious milestone: Hassan and Hussein's first birthday, 2 December 2010. (*Daragh McSweeney*)

Santa's Little Helpers! Hassan and Hussein with me, Christmas 2010. Miracles still happen, and dreams do come true … (*Crispin Rodwell*)

| THE SEPARATION SURGERY

I cried all the way over to the hospital while my sweet boys cooed and gurgled in their pram, looking up at me with their great big brown eyes. This was it; it was life or death now: the big one. I really didn't know where I was expected to find the strength to go through with what lay ahead. My hands shook on the pram as I wheeled the boys into their ward. Their room was the very last on the corridor, and as we passed the other parents and nurses it felt a little like a funeral procession. People who knew our situation nodded at me, lowered their eyes, or simply stopped to embrace me. It was such an overcast, rainy April day. I had to turn the light on in the boys' room as it was so bleak. I looked around at the sterile hospital walls and felt desperately afraid. I took out every card and photo I had brought with me and spent an hour covering those bare walls with beautiful images of love and support. I pinned up pictures of the boys and their sisters, heart-warming images of Iman's toothy grin and Malika's blinding smile. I pinned up pictures of them at the bike run, tried to paper over my fear with those images until the room became a little less sad, less hollow, less terrifying. Cards from all over Ireland, from Spain, New Zealand and the US were pinned together to make up a carefully constructed shrine for my boys. I had to do something to hold back my rising terror, had to keep busy. Finally, I took out the book of messages, pulled up a chair and read them out to my boys while fat, hot tears streamed down my cheeks. I couldn't bear to see the hands on the wall clock surging on and on like an unstoppable train, lunging towards our blackest hour. I felt my resolve weaken with every passing minute.

Later that afternoon Azzedine came over to the hospital and not long after he arrived there was a gentle rap on the door. It was the Imam, who had called by to bless the boys, the same Imam who had blessed them the day they were born. As soon as he started, they began to cry, so I picked them up in my arms to comfort them. The Imam took one look at my frightened face before touching my arm softly and saying: 'Trust in God, Angie, not the doctors.' I held fast to those words throughout that dreadful day. I tried to believe that no harm would come to my sons, but it was impossible to keep that creeping fear at bay. I feared for their lives with every intake of breath and felt my life would slip away with every exhalation.

When the blessing had finished, one of the nurses called by to tell me two big cardboard boxes had arrived for us and were waiting at the desk. One, I discovered, was from a Marisa Fragolini, a Cork dance teacher. I opened it to find it was absolutely stuffed with letters and cards from people at home. Marisa, whom I didn't even know at the time, had organised a fundraiser for the twins. All those involved, including little children, had written the most beautiful letters to us which she then posted over. The box was also filled with chocolates and sweets and crisps for the girls. I opened the second box to be greeted by an explosion of pink. Marisa had contacted another group in the UK called the Midlands Dance Company. She told them about our two girls, and they very kindly sent them fantastic pink ballet outfits with shoes and clips and just about everything a little girl could want. I couldn't believe this kindness; it was such a lovely gesture, which came at our lowest ebb. I decided to tell Malika and Iman that the boxes were a gift to them from the boys.

Just then Mr Kiely arrived and I noticed he was carrying the consent forms for us to sign so the surgery could go ahead the next day. I could see a sadness in his face as he asked me who was going to sign the forms. Azzedine and I looked at each other, neither one of us wanting to be the one to sign what could very possibly be a death sentence. Azzedine took our sons up in his arms and turned away, so we couldn't see his tears. As strong as my husband was, I knew he couldn't bear to sign those forms. He, just like me, wanted to wrap the boys up and leave that hospital. I told Mr Kiely that I would be the one to sign the forms, tears running down my cheeks. He sat down beside me and gently went through the risks involved in this massive procedure. He wrote down three words: bleeding, infection and death; these were the terrifying risks my babies faced. I looked at those awful words and wanted to just rip up those forms. He showed me where to sign, but how could I? I was their mother—I was meant to protect them! I paused for a moment, pen in hand, my hand shaking like a leaf. I thought to myself this was what was best for them, this was what they needed, and I signed them both: one for Hassan and one for Hussein. I knew if I followed my heart I would have torn them up and left my sons together, but I had to think with my head, think what was best for the boys. It took every ounce of strength I had to sign, but I had tremendous faith in God, in Mr Kiely and the team at GOSH. I knew the whole nation at home would be praying for Hassan and Hussein the following day and the power of that prayer would help them through their biggest challenge.

A couple of hours later Val brought the girls across to the hospital to say goodbye. They were enthralled by the mysterious boxes lying in the middle of the floor. I had promised them a little party with their brothers as I desperately wanted my girls to have some happy memories from that night in case it was the last time we would all be together. Malika's eyes lit up as she whispered,

'Mummy, what's in the boxes?' I said, 'You won't believe this but your brothers got you these fantastic presents as a special surprise!' I remember the light in her eyes as she pulled out those gorgeous costumes; it felt wonderful to see such innocent happiness and belief in all that's good amid that crushing fear.

I let the girls dress up while we lit some candles on a chocolate Smarties cake and sang good luck to the boys to the tune of 'Happy Birthday'. I held myself together with the last remaining strength I had while the girls were in the room, but it was as if I was holding back a surging river with a slowly crumbling wall. The girls were so excited; they ran down to the nurses' station and I heard them shouting, 'We have the best brothers in the world!' They dragged the staff up to share some cake and watch their improvised dance performance. The room was an absolute mess at this stage; Iman had chocolate cake all over her, there were sweets everywhere and bubble wrap all over the floor, but it was also exactly how I had wanted it.

Amid all that excitement and happiness and little girls' laughter, we almost forgot for a moment the agony that was awaiting us, waiting to bind us in its clammy, febrile grasp. I wanted to scream out at the top of my voice and shatter the glass in that clock. I wanted to stop its relentless ticking and just float there in that golden moment, watching my girls playing, smiling and laughing while my happy boys gurgled and cooed in their cot.

All too soon it was time for the girls to leave. I tried to keep my voice from cracking. I told them to kiss their brothers goodnight and held my breath and prayed for strength. I did not want them to witness my fear, but when Malika asked me, 'Mummy, when will I see my brothers again?' the floodgates finally burst open; I broke down. Her words pierced my frail heart. I didn't want to lie to her. I said, 'Please God, all going well, you will see them soon, when they are strong enough, sweetheart.' Iman was too young to understand anything; she was blissfully oblivious to what was coming. I told her to say goodbye to the boys and she did exactly as she had always done: leant over, kissed them both and shouted, 'Bye-bye Hassan. Bye-bye Hussein. Love you, see you later!' This time it killed me to hear her say those words, to watch her simply walk away without looking back. How could I possibly tell her that if something went wrong she would never see her brothers again, or that we had lost one of them? They had grown so attached to the boys over the previous four months. They loved every bit of them; in their innocence they never saw anything different about them. They loved them exactly as they were and saw no reason to change them. When Malika said goodbye to her brothers, I noticed she lingered just a bit longer than usual; a look of worry flashed across her face as she turned away from their cot. I hated that she knew there was something wrong; I hated the world at that moment for bringing fear into my little girl's heart. I bent down to give my daughters a hug. I knew the next time I would see them the surgery would have begun and it would be in God's hands.

It was bleak and quiet without the kids. It was almost 9 p.m. when they left and the ward had grown hushed. Our darkest hour began to bear down on us. One of the nurses wheeled in a second bed for us to sleep in, but I knew I would not sleep that night; I wondered if I would ever sleep again. As each member of staff finished their shift they came in to wish us luck. Mr Pat O'Brien called by to say goodbye and I desperately fought to remain composed, but I just could not stop crying as he bent over and kissed them both. It was as if the boys had captured everyone's heart; they all wanted them to come through this. The text messages and emails started to pour in from home as the night went on, such powerful words that reduced me to tears. So many people were thinking of the boys and that was an immense comfort. I remember some time after midnight Azzedine started trying to get me to sleep. I hadn't slept properly in a week; I had turned into a complete insomniac. The constant churning fear in my stomach used to keep me up all night. If I lay down for too long, my thoughts became like demons whispering in my ear, driving me mad. Azzedine begged me to put the boys down, but I just couldn't. I could see he was fighting fatigue—he kept dozing off and waking with a start—so I let him sleep. I put my sons under my arm and rocked them and kissed them all night long. I didn't plan to put them down, not for a moment; I didn't want to waste one second. The nurses came in and out intermittently throughout the night and would tell me to get some rest, but how could I? I knew it could be my last hold, my last kiss, my last cuddle.

Earlier in the night the boys had woken up, so I chatted to them for hours. I told them stories about their wonderful sisters and their amazing Dad. I told them how they were going to grow up to be big strong boys and we were going to love them and hold them and never let them go. When they fell asleep again I just watched them. They were simply gorgeous with their long, endless eyelashes. I was afraid I would never again get to feel their warmth, their hearts beating together, or hear their tiny baby sighs. I knew when this beautiful little bundle woke they would need plenty of love. I had to fast them overnight for the surgery, so I was going to be there when they opened their eyes.

All too soon dawn's unwelcome light started to peep through the window. I pulled the blind down and tried to shut it out. The boys woke up, hungry and upset, and soon their moans turned into cries. It was as if they somehow knew what was coming and they were crying in fear, a fear I couldn't comfort. There were no reassurances for this; there was nothing anyone could say to help. It is the worst moment in a parent's life—knowing you might never see your children alive again.

Finally, that dreadful morning came: wet, grey and bleak. It was as if the sun never rose at all. Azzedine awoke. He couldn't believe he had slept through the night, but I was glad that one of us had. I knew I would need him during that endless, hateful day. At 7 a.m. our nurse friends Mary and Mae and our clinical psychotherapist Kati came in to see us before they started their shifts at UCLH. They said they would stay with me until the twins were taken down, and I was grateful for their support. As we talked, a couple of surgeons in their scrubs walked into the room. As soon as I saw them my legs went from under me; I thought they were coming to get the boys. I cried, 'No, no, you're too early!' but they explained to me they were anaesthetists who had just come to talk us through the procedure; they weren't taking the boys just yet. I couldn't stop crying because I was so relieved they were not going to take them from me. I was not ready—not then, not ever. They told me somebody would come to tell us when we had to bring the boys down. I remember watching that hateful clock ticking; the second hand jumping closer to 8.30 a.m., ever nearer the surgery. I needed more time; I needed to be alone with them, but I had to try to stay strong. My phone kept beeping with a constant stream of messages; I could almost feel the pain and worry emanating from them.

Then, finally, the moment I had been dreading in the pit of my stomach during every waking moment of the previous four months arrived: it was time to hand over my sons. I remember asking the nurse to take a final picture of us with the twins before we went down. Everything seemed a little surreal from that point on, as if it were happening in slow motion: I could hear the blood pumping in my ears, the fear gurgling in my stomach. The nurses asked me if I wanted to wheel the boys down in their cot, but I told them I would carry them down. I wanted them to feel comforted and loved until the very last moment. Before I took them in my arms I put a pair of tiny football socks on them in case their feet would be cold during the surgery. I knew this was probably silly as they wouldn't be able to feel anything under anaesthetic, but I couldn't bear the thought of them being cold.

I bundled my babies up in my arms and we started to walk towards the theatre. I don't know how one leg moved in front of the other. All my instincts were screaming inside my head to turn around and just run. I remember the staff and doctors and parents of other sick children wishing us luck and looking at us in sympathy, but I wasn't really taking anything in; everything seemed to be happening at a great distance from us, a swirling mass of grief. I was locked in a world of pain. I remember turning the corner to the corridor and half noticing the documentary crew filming us, but I was so out of it I barely registered their presence. I know some people wanted the camera crew to go away and leave us alone, but we had got to know and trust the crew by then, and it didn't bother me. I knew by letting them film that painful moment I would at least have a record of the last time I held the boys alive if the worst happened. I also knew it could help other families in the future who might have to face what we were now staring at down the barrel of a gun.

The corridor leading down to the theatre seemed endless. I held the boys tight, close to my heart, not wanting to let go. Azzedine had his arm around me trying to hold me up, but my legs were just so heavy, like lead. There were a few times I had to stop—I didn't know if I could keep going. The one thing that struck me was how wide-eyed and innocent the boys looked; they were staring up at me and smiling; they had no idea where they were headed and I felt like a monster for what I was about to allow them to go through. I was their mother, yet here I was about to hand them over to be cut apart, after which I might not even get them back. I knew I was doing it for them, but I felt so bad that I had signed those forms. What if they didn't make it?

Mr Kiely had always talked plainly to me about the surgery; he told me exactly how it could go. I was under no illusion about the huge risk involved, but I had trust in him. I used to call him the twins' saviour, but those hateful three words—'bleeding', 'infection' and 'death'—ran through my head like an evil mantra. We knew he would give it his all, and I wanted to believe he could do it, but I also wanted to just run away—run out of there, draw in the fresh air, get on a plane and never take them near another hospital again.

When we got to the operating theatre the nurse had to check the boys' ID tags on their legs, so I had to take off their football socks. I held them in my hand all that day; they became my talisman of hope. One of the surgeons, Ellie, greeted me at the door, looked into my eyes and said quietly, 'It's time to take them now, Mum.' I remember at that moment I pulled them closer and just turned away from her. I couldn't hand them over; I just wailed and wailed for my children. I asked her if I could bring them in and say goodbye inside, but she said the whole place had been sterilised, so I had to hand them over there and then. I said to Azzedine, 'Daddy, kiss your boys,' which he did, tears streaming down his face. The last thing I said to my twins was 'Mummy and Daddy love you very much, boys; Malika and Iman love you; please come back to us.' When she took them from my arms I felt utter emptiness, as if my very heart and soul had been ripped from my body and was taken into that theatre to be put under the knife. It felt as if a lonely wind was blowing in the cavity where my heart had been. I saw one of the surgeons in the background look at me and gently beat his hand to his chest. He was telling me he knew how hard it was and that they would take care of them. I turned to Azzedine and held him tightly as the doors of the operating theatre closed. I cried as I had never cried before. Even looking back now, I feel that I lost something of myself that day, and have never got it back, as if some part of me died.

| AN ENDLESS DAY

W e were escorted back to the boys' room in silence, up a back stair to avoid the gathering media with their TV cameras and satellite vans. The room felt incredibly empty without the twins, an empty nest to which my baby birds might never return. It was so quiet: a hollow, deathly silence. I curled up on the small bed next to their cot and howled into a pillow. Azzedine tried to comfort me, tried to tell me to be strong, but I was in bits. My heart shattered the moment they lifted my boys out of my arms and I could almost feel its splintered pieces adrift in my bloodstream.

All day long, all I thought about were surgical instruments cutting through my babies. I could almost feel them cutting through my own bones; cutting through my sanity; tearing down its crumbling walls and in through my own desperate heart. It was far too much for a mother to bear. I held their little football socks tightly all day. I put their softness to my face and wiped away my tears with them. I didn't ask the doctors where they were going to start separating my boys because I just didn't want to know, yet I obsessed about it. I knew all too well the level of risk involved; if even the slightest thing went wrong, both of my babies could die. I had signed the papers, so I was the one who had authorised it to go ahead. I watched those hands ticking on the clock and kept thinking: 'At what point are they at now? Are they alive or are they dead?' It was absolute hell. It was beyond hell.

Azzedine and I drifted in this purgatorial nightmare all day. The TV was switched on in the boys' room and images of my sons kept flashing up on the screen on CNN and on the BBC. It was election time in London, but the twins' story seemed to dominate the news that day. I remember thinking once again: 'How did we get to this?' We were just a regular family from a small town in Cork and here we were going through the worst day of our lives and it was all over the television, and the world's media was outside the door attempting to capture our grief.

After a couple of hours of trying to deal with the initial shock of handing the boys over, we had to dust ourselves off and go back to check on our girls, to see if they were coping well. It had been one of our first nights away from them, and I was particularly worried about Malika. I knew she had an idea as to the gravity of the situation, so I was desperate to reassure her that everything was going to be OK. We had to ask GOSH security to escort us any time we wished to leave the hospital so we could use a secret exit and avoid the media. I was crying my eyes out as the lift descended to the ground floor of the hospital, and the big heavy doors groaned open. I had to quickly dry my tears, grit my teeth and put on a happy face for my children. It was difficult to pretend. As soon as we walked in Malika said, 'Mummy, are the brothers gone down?' I just caught her and held her and sobbed into her hair. She took my hand and said, 'Mummy, don't worry, it's not going to hurt them!' I looked at my brave little girl and felt blessed to have her. I said, 'Yes, love, you're right. Nothing is going to hurt them now.' I wished I could really believe my own words, wished it was fairy dust they were sprinkling on my poor boys and I would wake to find it had all been a terrible nightmare.

That afternoon my sister Shirley and brother Chris arrived in London to support us. Azzedine and I, zombie-like, went back and forth to the hospital to wait for news on the boys. I recall at one stage the documentary crew approached us to say they would have to meet us to do some filming. It really was the last thing I wanted; I just didn't feel able for it. I was comforted by my nurse friends from UCLH who called by to see us at various points throughout the day, but because I hadn't eaten or slept in days, I could barely speak. I felt as if I were at war with myself: half of me wanted to keep strong for my girls and boys, while the other half just wanted to shut down completely.

I remember Mae Nugent called to the apartment and l let her in. I was very happy to see her and I do remember embracing her and then this blackness falling again. I was later told that a couple of moments after she sat down, I got up again and said, 'Oh Mae, I didn't know you were here!' and hugged her again. Everybody looked at me as if I had lost my mind, and now I can see I was so traumatised that I was not in my right senses at all.

Finally, at around 4 p.m., there was a knock on the door of the flat. It was the ward sister—I felt my stomach lurch. I couldn't read her expression. I desperately searched her face for some sign of what was to come but I could find none. She said, 'You need to come over now, Angie, the surgeons want to speak with you both.' I felt my insides turn over and this terrible fear run its icy fingers down my spine. I thought: 'This is it. This is when they are going to tell me my babies are dead.' I heard a shrieking inside my head. Azzedine held me as we crossed the street to the hospital, which loomed like a prison over us.

As we approached the boys' room, we saw there were about five surgeons, all in their gowns, waiting for us and I felt like running away. I was so convinced the boys were gone; I felt their loss deep inside me. The more we walked towards the surgeons, the longer the corridor seemed—darker and longer with each step. Azzedine was always strong for me, but I could see how terrified he was. I remember a look of fear etched across his face like a grimace. It felt as if we were hurtling towards a fatal car crash that there was no way of avoiding. I kept thinking: 'If the five of them are here, then obviously the boys are not.'

One of the surgeons, Mr Peter Kuckow, came over and told us to sit down and closed the door behind us. I couldn't sit down; I was frozen to the spot. Azzedine and I just stood there, holding one another, shaking and crying, waiting for the walls to come crashing in. Mr Kuckow smiled and said, 'You can relax. I'm not here to give you bad news—it's all going very well!' I almost fainted with relief as he explained to us that when they opened the boys up, they found a second gall bladder. This was incredible. I couldn't believe it. I said, 'But, there was no second gall bladder?' Mr Kuckow just nodded at me. I cried out, 'Well, then God himself must have put it there, because I know there was only one!' I was totally shocked by this news. The previous week there had been many tests carried out by many doctors in search of this second gall bladder. I was there—I saw the scans with my own eyes and there was only one. It was amazing that they had found another one; they were finding things they had never expected to discover, but there was still a long way to go. I was so relieved that my little boys were fighting on.

Mr Kuckow came to see us again at around 7 p.m.; we were terrified once more, anticipating bad news, but he said, 'Relax, I told you I would only come up if it was good news!' I felt I had been under water holding my breath and somebody had turned on my oxygen mask. About a half hour later we were told we had to do an update for the documentary. I don't really have any memory of this taking place, but looking back at the film now it seems as if I had left my body; I hardly recognise myself. Minutes seemed infinite and hours seemed like days. The clock that had hurtled forward with relentless force the previous night now seemed to hit the same second over and over again, heralding the most endless of days.

At about 10.45 p.m. that night we were informed that Mr Kiely himself wanted to see us. This was it. The nursing staff had told us the surgery had finished, but there was no reaction on the staff's faces; it was impossible to tell if it had been a success or not. As Mr Kiely walked towards us, I felt my legs turning to jelly. The ward sister and some of the other nursing staff, who had stayed with us long after their shifts had finished, left the room so we could speak to him. I remember hearing Mr Kiely say in his lovely reassuringly soft voice, 'You can relax now, they are separated, they are alive; it couldn't have gone any better.' Azzedine and I just fell to the floor in floods of tears; the relief felt like nothing I had ever experienced before. We just held each other and sobbed. I thanked God for his mercy while happiness, sadness and relief coursed through my veins. He told us the exact time of separation was 8 p.m.; that was the moment they were put on two separate trolleys and wheeled away to be worked on by two different teams. Hearing this made my heart ache for my beautiful boys; my sons who had come into this world together had been torn apart and were now struggling for life alone. It hurt to think of them apart like that, my little heart-shaped angels broken in two like my own shattered heart. Before Mr Kiely left us he reminded us it was still early days and it was one thing getting them out of surgery alive but yet another to get them out of intensive care.

Later that night Mr Kiely finished working on Hassan first and he was sent back to the Paediatrics Intensive Care Unit (PICU) ward while Prof Pierro finished Hussein. We were so blown away by the news that they had survived that we went back to the flat and gently took our sleepy little girls out of their beds. We held them to us as we told them their brothers were alive. Malika burst out crying with relief. We then shared the good news with Val and other family members and everyone was incandescent with happiness and relief.

Finally, we got the call that we were allowed to see the boys at about 2.30 a.m. Azzedine didn't want us to go that night; he wanted me to have a good night's sleep and then go to see them the following day. As I had not slept in 48 hours he was concerned as to how I would cope with the shock of seeing them separated, seeing my babies in separate cots for the first time, swollen, puffy and unconscious. He worried I wouldn't be able for it because of the state of exhaustion I was in, but I had to see my boys. When I had been reunited with them after their birth, I swore I would never be parted from them again. I told Azzedine I couldn't wait until morning; I had to see them, and see for myself that they were alive and that they were actually separated. So shortly afterwards we shuffled into the lift for the PICU ward. I remember walking past the nurses' station and turning the corner towards where the boys were. Azzedine and I held on to one another for dear life. The staff congratulated us on the boys' survival and stopped to embrace us. It had been by far the worst day of our lives, but when we found out the boys had survived it had quickly turned into the best.

Just as we were about to go in, I took Azzedine's hand and asked him to wait. 'I can't go in!' I said, tears brimming in my eyes. He replied, 'But I don't understand, you wanted to see them?' I told him I needed to take some time before going through those doors. The staff nurse told us that when we went into the room, Hassan would be on the left and Hussein on the right. I felt comforted that they had kept the boys in the same position they had always been in. I took three really deep breaths, which made my head spin for a moment, and desperately tried to summon the strength from somewhere to go and face what was behind those doors.

We walked in and the first thing I saw was all this machinery; there were so many tubes attached to my tiny little babies who were now in two huge cots. Azzedine and I just looked at each other; our jaws dropped in shock. I stood there looking from one baby to the other and thinking to myself: 'Where are my boys gone?' I was used to them being together snuggled up in their cots, and now we were looking at two very different little boys who were puffy and bruised and 6 ft apart. They were heavily sedated and two ventilators were breathing for them; they were unrecognisable. I noticed there were two signs on the end of the boys' cots. One read 'My name is Hassan and I'm the blue twin' and the other said 'I'm Hussein and I'm the green twin'. When the boys were born it was the same way; all their machines were labelled with either blue or green stickers. The two Munster rugby bibs that my sister had brought us were hanging off the end of each cot.

Azzedine and I went to Hussein first, as he was nearest. It is incredibly difficult to put into words what it felt like to go to one twin and for the other not to be there. The doctors had covered the boys with a sheet right up to their necks so we didn't have to see what they had been through. I turned to look at Hassan, my bright little active boy, now swollen and unrecognisable. I remember slipping my little finger into his hand and just wanting so much for him to squeeze it, or something, but there was no response. My sons couldn't see or hear me; they couldn't open their eyes and I couldn't communicate with them or tell them that Mummy and Daddy were there and would always be there.

The nurses tried to explain to me what all the machinery was for, but that night it seemed like way too much to take in. I just couldn't cope with it. We stayed at the boys' bedsides for the best part of two hours, just wanting to be there for them, even though we knew they weren't aware of our presence. We took some photographs even though it was incredibly hard to take pictures of them in that state, but I had to do it to convince myself they were really alive and separated. I needed to show Malika too that her brothers were alive. I knew it would mean everything to her to see the two boys in separate cots because it would be weeks before I could bring her to them. It just didn't seem right that they were separated. It was normal to see them joined, but not normal to see them apart.

It was very hard to tear ourselves away from them that night, but we were mentally and physically drained. The nurse told me

I could kiss them, but I was scared I would hurt them. Their lips, their faces—everything was so puffed up; you could tell just by looking at them what they had been through. I gently kissed them on their heads and the gorgeous warmth of their skin comforted me a little. Even though they seemed completely lifeless I could feel life in them still. We went back to the flat at around 4 a.m. and fell into a deep, dreamless sleep.

When I woke up it was hard to believe what had happened. I just kept flicking back and forth through the photos I had taken. My boys, now separated, were still fighting on together. That morning it was as if the whole world wanted to know if the twins were alive. From around 8 a.m. my phone beeped ceaselessly. The press office at GOSH was inundated with calls, and they told us we needed to get a statement out as soon as possible to hold off the giant wave of media interest that was bearing down on all of us. We were asked if we would like Mr Kiely to do a press conference on the steps of the hospital to update the media on the boys' progress, but I thought he had been through enough and it would have been unfair of us to expect him to do that. Instead we decided we would release a statement through the hospital. The communications department offered to prepare it, but we wanted it to be personal and from the heart. After all, we had received many hundreds of cards from people all over the world so this was a way of answering them. We knew many people at home in Ireland had stayed up all night praying and waiting for news. The whole place was holding its breath for news and I found it overwhelming that all these people had taken my boys to their hearts and were wishing them well and worrying for them. I remember feeling strung out from exhaustion and just staring out the window of our apartment at a glorious, golden day, so bright and warm. Everything was dappled in sunlight. I felt the sun was smiling down on us after what had been one of the most miserably wet, cold days I ever lived through. I picked up a pen and paper and just started to write. I wrote:

The sun is shining today for our two little fighters, who have won the battle of their lives. Words cannot express the relief and love we feel for our two boys. We thank God, we thank the surgeons and the gifted team at Great Ormond Street Hospital, and we thank from the bottom of our hearts the Irish nation and everyone who prayed for our beloved twins. We are so proud of the courage and strength that Hassan and Hussein have shown, and they both have made the world a much better place with them in it.

Everyone loved the statement and I was happy at the way it was picked up by the media, so celebratory. I had been confused and disorientated the day before but that morning my mind was as crystal clear as the impossibly blue sky outside my window. Azzedine rang his family in Algeria; they had been praying around the clock for the boys and were very happy for us. They had seen only images of the boys online or from the photographs we had sent them, and it was difficult for his family being so far away from it all. Azzedine never stopped praying for the boys; his way of looking at it was just because you get what you want doesn't mean you stop there. You must keep giving thanks—always.

I put on a nice summer dress and dressed the girls in special tee-shirts we had got made, depicting the boys, with the words 'Our Little Fighters' written on them. I brushed my hair and put some make-up on my gaunt, pale face. Azzedine put on a suit and we headed out into the sunshine hand in hand. The sun warmed my face. Spring was in the air and in my step.

The night before, I had said to Azzedine that if the boys survived the operation, I would get down on my hands and knees and kiss the ground outside the hospital. He thought I was just joking, so that next day as we passed the hospital I looked at Azzedine and said, 'Remember what I told you yesterday? Well, watch this!' at which point I got down on my hands and knees and I kissed the ground and thanked God for saving my children. A woman from the Cayman Islands whom I had met in the laundry room of the hospital during the week walked by and saw me. I told her the boys were alive and she gave me a big hug. People said to me the boys were put on this earth for a reason; they had survived so much already in their brief lives; they had been through so much from birth to separation and I remember thinking that morning: 'My God, when I named them my Little Fighters back in August how little I knew then just what a fight they would have.'

The four of us and my family members who had come to London took a triumphant stroll down a sun-soaked Great Ormond Street. Along the way we met some reporters from home as well as some of the other parents from the hospital, all of whom stopped to congratulate us. The postman handed me an enormous bundle of cards from people at home. The sun beat down as the girls skipped and laughed. We all held hands and breathed in the beautiful air of hope. It seemed a long time since we had been able to do that—just breathe in life and breathe out happiness. We had had such a tough year; we knew things could have been a whole lot different if the boys hadn't survived, so at that very moment we felt both lucky and grateful. To know our boys had survived was a feeling I could never do justice to with words. Even though we knew they weren't out of the woods yet, we also knew they were more than halfway there.

As we carried on down the road a photographer approached us and asked us how we felt, raising his camera up to photograph us. I remember just throwing my arms up in the air and thinking to myself: 'They did it!' It turned out to be such a wonderful, joyous image, it still makes me cry to look at that photograph today. I saw the light had returned to Malika's eyes; it was good to see her look so happy again. Relief washed over us like a blissful dive into a still ocean but we knew the boys' battle was far from over.

Chapter 14 ～

APART—BUT TOGETHER FOREVER

When the initial excitement began to die down later that day, it really started to hit home just what was ahead of the boys. Although we had seen them the night before, we had been so exhausted and overcome with relief that we barely registered anything besides the fact that they were separated and alive. It was the next day that the cold realisation hit me that we were only halfway up that treacherous and unpredictable mountain. We left the gorgeous sunshine and celebrations behind and went back into the oppressive heat of the intensive care ward. I felt such a deep and overwhelming sadness to see my tiny boys unconscious, swollen and frail, clinging to life like little baby birds. We had grown so accustomed to seeing their bright brown eyes dancing with life in front of us that it was utterly devastating to see them lifeless, fighting for life alone.

Mr Kiely told us they would remain under heavy sedation for about two weeks, so we knew we had another agonising wait ahead of us. We also knew that getting them out of intensive care free of infection was going to be a serious challenge as they had big open wounds running from their chests to their pelvises. There were no skin grafts or plastic surgery or artificial ribs for my boys, as some of the media reported at the time. Their wounds remained completely open. We were told that because a baby's skin is malleable and supple, the best way to close up the wounds would be to gradually pull the skin back together and tuck it in piece by piece. There was a kind of mesh holding them together internally, but until their wounds were closed up there was quite a significant risk of infection.

When Azzedine and I would go to see them, the nurses would place a sheet over them so we wouldn't have to see what lay beneath: a thin layer of gauze lay between us and utter horror. I didn't want to see their wounds at all at first; I just couldn't look. I didn't think I would ever be able to bear seeing the pain they had been through as they lay there motionless in their cots. Every time the nurses came to change their dressings, we would leave the room. I remember catching glimpses of their soiled dressings, saturated with blood, and I would feel as if my own poor heart would burst from the pain of it. As much as I tried not to, I couldn't help imagining what their wounds looked like. Azzedine insisted I not look at them. He told me the boys were sedated, and that they wouldn't feel anything, but I worried greatly that they could. The care the boys received at GOSH was so meticulous and constant that it was a reassurance, but for that entire two weeks before they began to open their eyes I felt as if my whole body was clenched in a vice; I could not sleep or eat and I barely dared to breathe until I could hold my sons again.

As the days went by we started to get a little more used to the intensive care unit, but it was impossible to ever feel anything but highly stressed in that liminal place between death and life, where at any moment alarm sounds would herald the end of a child's life. It was such a scary place for a parent. One afternoon the silence was broken by this sudden, shrill alarm coming from a bed just a few feet from my boys. I looked on in horror as doctors and nurses ran about desperately fighting to save a child, but to no avail. I ran to the bathroom and howled for that child and for his parents and for my own boys and for every child who ever felt a moment's pain in this world. I shall never forget it for the rest of my life; I still find it hard to think about it today and I feel such intense sadness for the little one's devastated parents. I would sit by my boys' bedside and my eyes would ache from being constantly trained on their monitors, watching with dread every changing number, every flashing light, every beep and every sound. It felt as if I were holding my breath all day just waiting for something to go wrong. Each and every time their monitors beeped my heart would thump in my chest. We were constantly on edge, constantly anxious for their lives. An alarm would sound and I would think: 'Oh God, please no! Don't take them from me, not now.' It was so much worse that we were watching over two children, fearing for the lives of two precious babies. The worry and fear was relentless; it lived in our blood. It never left me, not for one second.

On the third day after their separation I walked into their room and stopped dead in my tracks. I looked at Hassan and whatever way his sheet had moved all I saw was this hollow where his leg should be. This was really the first time that it struck me just how much hardship was awaiting my boys. I looked from one of my sons to the other, noticing how the gauze sheets that covered their tiny bodies came to a sharp and heartbreaking drop where their legs should have been. As they had only half a pelvis each, the hollow was all the more pronounced, all the more painful to look at. I remember thinking: 'My God, half of my babies are gone!' and bursting into tears. When they were joined, even though they had one leg each, they somehow looked balanced, but after they were separated and their pelvis was halved it was such as shock. I stood over them with tears streaming down my face. It looked as if a magician had come and sawed my babies in half, but this was no magic trick or illusion. This was real. I was tortured by it, but I had to just swallow my fear and learn to accept it; there was always going to be another stage with the twins, always another mountain to climb.

As time passed, Azzedine and I began to feel more and more helpless. Our lives consisted of going back and forth to the hospital and simply staring at monitors and listening to the bleeps. There was nothing we could do to help our boys. We felt very much out of the picture when it came to their care and longed to do something to help our sons, who were fighting for life so bravely. Ever mindful of our feelings, the wonderful staff at the PICU ward sensed our increasing frustration so they taught us how to keep the boys' mouths and eyes moist, which at least gave us a sense that we were helping in some small way. One of the nurses asked us if we would like to participate in the dressing of their wounds, but Azzedine said no, it would be far too painful for us to bear, and I agreed. One evening, when I was just about to leave to go over to the girls, I bent down to kiss Hussein goodbye on the head when my motion caused the sheet to lift off his body. I came face to face with my son's angry, open wound. I screamed in pain, but no sound came out. It looked as if a shark had come and bitten a huge chunk out of my baby's stomach, and the wound was gaping open. I couldn't believe what I had seen. I felt my head start to spin. The sadness and fear brought a metallic taste to my mouth. I couldn't understand how he was alive and breathing with such a massive wound running from his chest to his lower abdomen. I ran from the hospital in tears and told Azzedine what I had seen. I was inconsolable; I wanted desperately to swap places with my boys. How could they endure something so terrible and be so tiny and innocent? Azzedine begged me not to think of it, but it haunted me that whole night. I couldn't erase that image from my mind, couldn't bear the fact that they had been through such agony and yet still they had a huge fight ahead of them.

As I had only a quick glimpse of the wound, my mind started to play tricks on me. I couldn't tell if the image in my mind was completely real or imagined. I am naturally squeamish, and before the twins were born I would almost faint at the sight of blood, but now that I had that image burned in my mind, I knew I had to do something. I awoke the following morning and told Azzedine that I had made a decision: I was going to look at both of their wounds. Azzedine thought it a really bad idea; he told me it would be far too traumatic, but I told him I had to see the wounds properly for myself and understand what they meant. I also felt I would then be able to monitor how well they were progressing. I might then be able to understand exactly what they had gone through and where they needed to get to in order to recover. I knew I had to get stronger for my boys, face it head-on, ask questions and do everything in my power to help them through.

I was petrified as I waited for the nurses to come. The curtains were drawn around the boys. Azzedine left the cubicle and I was shown Hassan's wounds first and then Hussein's. I gasped as I looked on this horrifying vision of what my sons had been through. I cried my heart out; it was just as ghastly as I had imagined. I almost felt their pain; I wished I could take it away. Hussein's wound was particularly nasty; it was weeping a lot and it was very slow to heal.

Mr Kiely came by to check on the boys one afternoon and told the nurses that they should sprinkle some brown sugar on it. I thought he was joking, but I saw from his expression that he was totally serious. I went to the canteen to get some sugar but it was a Sunday so the coffee shop was closed. I left the hospital and went straight down to the local Starbucks and just grabbed a stash of sugars and marched back up to the hospital. I realise now I must have seemed very odd to the people in Starbucks, but I was so focused on trying to help my little boy that I wasn't even thinking about anything else. We sprinkled the sugar on the wound and like magic within a few days it was much improved.

Every two days the boys were brought down to theatre to have a couple of centimetres of their skin closed up. They surgeons would pull the skin together over the wound and tuck it in, and then leave it in for a few days before doing it again. I was fearful every time they went down to surgery that something would go wrong. I paced the halls like a madwoman, the taste of fear in my mouth and that awful hospital smell invading my senses. I knew an infection could have killed them and I lived and breathed that fear day in and day out. One afternoon, when they were closing up part of Hussein's wound, his heart rate dropped dramatically. I was so scared we would lose him. For two days we didn't know if he would pull through. I prayed and begged God to let him live. After two days he recovered but, just as we were about to draw breath again, the following day Hassan's lungs collapsed suddenly while he was in theatre at the final stages of closing up his wound. The doctors came down to tell us what had happened. I was convinced our happy ending was going to be over. I once again heard that shrieking in my head and nothing coming out of my mouth. Hassan was put on an oscillator, which breathed for him, and for two days nobody could tell us whether he would pull through or not.

Every passing second of uncertainty felt life a lifetime. I felt so helpless; I could do nothing to help my frail son who was clinging to life, but pray and beg God to let him live. I thought: 'How many more times can my heart take this? Will it just stop beating from the sheer force of this grief?' It was like a game of Russian roulette all the time: one moment they were alive, the next they could be cruelly snatched from us as fast as a bullet from a gun. I was incredibly hurt when I later heard that during this period of utter anguish a member of the media at home was talking about us, saying we were not giving enough updates on the boys' progress! In that week alone we nearly lost our two sons and the last thing we had on our minds was a media update. We didn't even know ourselves whether they were going to live or die! Nobody seemed to understand the distress and fear we were living with every second of every day.

The hospital released a statement to the media two weeks after the boys' surgery.

A Great Ormond Street Hospital spokesperson said:

'The two boys remain in intensive care. They are stable and making progress daily. The surgical team had always anticipated a substantial period of recovery from this major surgery. They are broadly where the medical team expected them to be at this point.'

Angie Benhaffaf, mother of Hassan and Hussein said:

'The past two weeks have been extremely tough for our "little fighters" and for me, Az and the girls. Even though the sun has shone since their separation, we've also had dark clouds that hovered over their little cots in intensive care and brought difficult days for them both. Both Hassan and Hussein have been through so much. We know there is still a long journey ahead. As parents we sometimes feel helpless and we watch anxiously what our precious twins are going through every day.

'The one thing that is helping us to get through each new day is the support we are still getting from the public, and the bundles of post that come twice a day for the boys at GOSH. Thanks to each of you who continue to keep the boys in your thoughts and prayers. Also, a big thank you to the media for once again allowing us to have this precious time with our "little fighters!"'

Little by little the doctors began to reduce the boys' morphine dosages in the hope that they would start to wake up naturally. I will never forget how heartbreaking it was to see my two babies suffer the symptoms of morphine withdrawal. They would shake violently and I could see they were crying in pain, but as they were on a ventilator with tubes going down their throats it prevented them from making any sound. I will never, until my dying day, forget the anguish I felt at seeing my little boys' faces screwed up in pain, but hearing no sound come from them. It was like watching a baby crying on television with the sound muted. I was scared that I would never hear their cries again, and for quite some time I actually believed I never would.

Malika began attending the school at GOSH, in which I had enrolled her before we left Ireland, and it was lovely to see her setting off in the mornings with her packed lunch, smiling and waving to me. I felt relieved that she had an outlet away from us, away from the pain and worry she must have sensed from her parents. I loved picking her up after her classes and listening to her excitingly babble about what a fantastic day she had. It reminded me of collecting her from school at home in Cork and walking beside her as she excitedly told me about her day. Just for those couple of minutes I would be momentarily transported back to a time before all of this, before we knew the boys were conjoined, before our lives were invaded by fear. Malika was proud to sign in every day as Hassan and Hussein's sister; she was always proud of them and never resentful of the fact that because of her brothers she had to leave her friends and her home and be brought to a small, cramped flat in London where her mother constantly cried and her father always looked worried.

As the weeks went on I could tell from Malika's questions that she was getting pretty anxious about the twins and was dying to see them. Finally, about three weeks after the separation, we started to prepare the girls for a visit. It had been such a shock for us to see them, so we knew what a huge shock it would be for a child and such a difficult thing for them to comprehend. I did my best to explain how the doctors had separated them and that they were now in two separate cots and were no longer 'stuck together'. Malika said, 'Mummy, I am going to have to draw them a picture each because now they have two cots, so they will need one each!' I told her that was a great idea; she drew two gorgeous pictures for them and coloured them exactly the same way, one for Hassan and one for Hussein.

On a cloudy Saturday afternoon we took the girls by the hand and asked them to come and see the boys. I felt really nervous of how they would react. We had asked one of the nurses to capture the moment on video and as we turned the corner to see them I held my breath and hoped the girls wouldn't be upset. Malika had just turned six and Iman was nearly three at the time and yet I noticed with a tinge of sadness how much they had adapted to hospital life. They rubbed the Spirogel on their hands almost automatically and looked up at my worried face as if to say, 'It's ok, Mummy, we are ready.' I pushed open the door and told them that Hussein was in the first cot while Hassan was in the other but they were asleep so they needed to be very quiet. The girls just flew into the room and immediately began trying to climb up on Hussein's cot to get a look at him. Azzedine and I were frightened and started shouting, 'Don't touch that, be careful!' We lifted the girls up to let them have a look at their brother; thankfully by this stage the boys were no longer puffy or ill-looking so it wasn't such a shock for them. I held Iman close and said, 'Now look, Iman, this is your brother Hussein.' Her jaw literally dropped as she looked at him, then at Malika and back to me. She said, 'Mummy, where is Hassan gone?' I replied, 'Look, Iman, Hassan is over there!' and I pointed to the other cot, but she said, 'No, no, Hassan is gone! Hassan is gone!' tapping the pillow space next to Hussein's head where Hassan would have been. I tried to reassure her by saying, 'No, sweetheart, Hassan is over there and I am going to bring you over to him next,' at which I carried her over to Hassan's cot, but she just couldn't grasp the fact that they were separated at all. As soon as we got to Hassan's cot she started to point and say, 'Mummy, where's Hussein gone?' It took her many weeks to fully understand that the boys weren't 'stuck together' any more.

The following day we brought the girls over to see them again and as we stood there silently gazing at our two amazing boys, the nurses surprised us by asking if we wanted to hold our sons. I was gobsmacked. I badly wanted to hold them—I ached for it—but I was also nervous that I would hurt them. I hadn't held them in two weeks, but they were hooked up to ventilators and machines so I was hardly able to touch them. Azzedine started making excuses because he was afraid. He said, 'Oh no, there are too many tubes. It would be too much trouble,' but he caught a glimpse of my expression and immediately saw that I was dying to hold my babies. So the nurses moved a big sofa between the two cots and told us to sit down. Then slowly and carefully they took my gorgeous boys from their cots with their tubes and wires attached and put Hassan into Azzedine's arms and Hussein in mine. Our two little girls held up their milk feeds as we held the boys. None of us spoke; we just stared down at our sleeping babies. I was speechless with happiness. It was such a wonderful moment. Although we were scared to move, it was still incredible to hold them as two separate babies for the very first time. It was strange looking down at Hussein and not seeing Hassan and then looking across at Hassan and not seeing Hussein. It was like getting to know two babies all over again. It was new and amazing. I could tell immediately how busy things were going to get now that they were separated! I felt Hussein's warmth in my arms and it gave me such strength to feel life in his veins.

Three weeks had passed since their separation, so we had to say goodbye to Val who was returning home to Ireland. We were on our own again. It was such an impossibly difficult time as we had to cope with all these life-threatening decisions and situations on our own because when I was with the girls Azzedine was at the hospital and vice versa. It's hard to put into words just how relentlessly draining it is to sit by your two sons' bedsides day after day and fear for their lives with every breath. We would have found the whole situation impossible if it was not for our nurse friends Mary and Mae, who would come and take the girls out to allow Azzedine and me to spend some precious time together with the boys. I was also hugely grateful to Vodafone, who called us up a week before the surgery and topped up my phone with €1,000 of credit, which meant when I was in the hospital and Azzedine was with the girls I could phone him any time without having to worry about astronomical roaming charges. These simple acts of kindness meant the world to us.

A couple of days later I started to notice the boys' eyelids flicker and blink so we knew that they were trying to wake up. I remember looking at them and seeing those bright brown eyes open and look back at me and thinking how they were far too young to have gone through so much. The first time Hassan opened his eyes I said, 'Hello, my gorgeous boy. Mummy is here now and I will never leave your side; you just rest and get better.' Soon Hussein started to wake up and I thanked God that my boys were coming back to life before my very eyes, like little flowers unfurling.

The next big step was to get them off their TPN feeding lines, which were keeping them nourished while they were unconscious, and then the doctors began to discuss taking them off their ventilators. This really worried me as it was going to test whether the boys could breathe unassisted as separated twins. There was a big risk they simply wouldn't be able to breathe alone. We worried about it night and day. The day they took Hassan off his ventilator, Tuesday, 27 April, I had to leave the ward—I couldn't bear to watch. I paced the corridor for an hour. I was tortured by the thought that my boy wouldn't be able for it. All these dreadful scenarios raced through my head as I paced and paced. Eventually, I couldn't stand the uncertainty any more, so I crept back to the boys' room just as they had successfully taken him off. They fitted him with the little CPAP tubes again to give him some breathing assistance and he did very well. I just burst out crying with relief. The next day Hussein came off his ventilator successfully. I couldn't believe our luck. My Little Fighters were coming back to me!

Chapter 15 ～

| A HERO'S WELCOME HOME

I had been looking forward to doing some clothes shopping for my boys now that they were separated. This was a fresh start for them and I was dying to do what I had never been able to do before and that was just pick out any little outfit I desired without having to check if there were press fasteners or buttons. Finally, I would no longer have to take things out of the packaging to see if they would fasten together. One afternoon Azzedine and I got the tube into central London and headed to the Disney store on Oxford Street. I felt like a child in a sweet shop; it was just so liberating to be able to walk into a store and browse like all the other Mums, picking out anything I wanted in the twins' size. I fell in love with two beautiful Disney outfits and I just couldn't wait to go back and dress the boys in them. I had waited five months to dress my sons separately! For the first time, too, I was able to buy babygrows that had buttons on the back! Such inconsequential things like this meant the world to me back then; everything was new and full of joy. Many times I'd had to walk past adorable outfits that I would have loved to have bought for my sons but I knew they would not work for conjoined twins. Now that they were separated, I no longer obsessed about dressing them differently to emphasise their individuality; now I could dress them in the same, cute outfits. I bought them a set of matching babygrows and hats that day and just couldn't wait to get back. I took such pleasure in putting their new outfits into two separate drawers; one by Hussein's cot and one by Hassan's.

One afternoon I brought Malika over to see her brothers after school. It was just the two of us in the room and I remember her chatting away to Hussein, telling him all about her new school and her day when she suddenly stopped and fell silent. The babies were dressed in two little vests and, as it had been incredibly warm in the intensive care unit that day, we had taken their blankets off them. This was the first time that Malika had really seen the boys from head to toe since their separation. Noticing she had fallen silent, I turned to her and saw that she was looking at both boys very intently, running her eyes over them. Suddenly she said, 'Mummy, I can see the legs now,' to which I replied, 'What do you mean, sweetheart?' She looked at me with tears in her eyes and said, 'Mummy, I can see their legs are missing now.' I tried desperately not to show her the pain I was in as I said, 'But we always knew that, love,' to which she replied, 'Yes, I know, but I just wish they could grow another leg each.' My heart sank. I said to her, 'But don't you remember meeting that lady, Heather, sweetheart—the lady with the pretend leg?' She nodded in response, big tears welling in her brown eyes. 'Well, she told me that one day these guys are going to swim much faster than you. You wait and see. You have two legs, so you have more weight to carry, but they have only one leg each, so they will be little flyers, much faster than you!' She looked at me, incredulous for a moment, and then gave a big, wide smile and laughed at the top of her voice. I was relieved. From time to time she would say to me how it made her sad that the boys had only one leg each, but I would tell her they were going to get two new superhero legs one day and were going to walk and run and chase her around the park. I told her that a fairy had told me they would need a big sister like her to help them walk on their magic legs, and my gorgeous girl would look at me full of wonder.

When the twins were joined I had always covered up the fact that they had only one leg each. Every time we took them out I would wrap them tightly in a blanket so nobody could tell, but now that they were getting better and stronger I knew it wouldn't be long before they were out of intensive care. It was time to let people know. I thought long and hard about how we would do this and finally decided that as we were still filming the documentary, I would ask Mr Kiely if he would be the one to reveal it. The film crew planned to interview him the following day, and I thought it would be the perfect time to bring it up. I wanted it done in a very matter-of-fact way and I knew I was far too emotional to do it.

Later, when the documentary was aired, I felt very anxious because I knew it was going to be the first time that we would reveal the boys were missing limbs, but the way Mr Kiely dealt with it was hugely dignified. As he was being interviewed he just said the boys were joined from chest to pelvis; they shared a liver, chest, bladder and gut and they had one leg each. That was it; he said it very casually, almost like an afterthought, so there was no real issue made of it. The media handled it very sensitively too the next day in their coverage of the documentary; nobody made a big deal out of it and I didn't have to worry about keeping it a secret any more. I wanted to banish secrecy from our lives altogether; there was going to be no more sneaking around and hiding the truth. At least now, I thought, we might be able to get on with our lives in peace. I no longer wanted to feel frightened that someone would find something out about my boys. I was incredibly proud of them and not prepared to hide away their shining light any more.

As soon as the documentary had finished that night my phone began to buzz relentlessly; hundreds of text messages began to pour in from people, full of positivity. Many told me they had sobbed watching it and I don't think I stopped crying once myself. Watching the moment where we handed over the boys for surgery was very painful viewing. I sobbed the whole way through it. I hoped that we, in some way, helped to alter people's perception of conjoined twins, and how society views these babies as a whole. I wanted to show the world that conjoined twins are just as beautiful and special as any twins, and I sincerely hope when the next pair are born, people will think of the two little boys from Ireland who were so lovely and fought so hard for life. I hope we have shown how beautiful and special they are, a wonderful gift that brings light and joy to an often cruel and jaded world.

Mr Kiely always had such incredible faith in our boys. He came to us the day they were taken off their ventilator and told us he believed it would not be long before they would be able to breathe completely unaided. He said they could be back in a surgical ward within a week. I could not believe what I was hearing. I remember some of the other doctors saying it would take a lot longer, but the Little Fighters went one better and were out just days after that conversation took place. They had been on CPAPS for only two days when they began to breathe on their own, just three and a half weeks after their separation. It was nothing short of a miracle how quickly they recovered; I kept waiting for something to go wrong, but it just kept getting better and better. I hardly dared to believe it.

They left the PICU ward on 1 May and went back to a surgical ward. I couldn't hold my tears as they were wheeled out into the light. It was truly one of the happiest days of our lives. I filmed the journey from intensive care to the Woodland Ward, my little boys smiling up at me with their dancing eyes. It was such a celebratory moment, full of light, full of hope. All the other parents were hugging us and kissing us and we were jumping for joy. The nurses put the boys in their new cots and I remember laughing as the girls ran from one to the other all afternoon; it was such fun. I loved every second of caring for them. As hard and exhausting as it was, it was such a joy to see them alive and crying and causing a fuss. I realised that it had been more than a month since the boys had really seen one another, so I asked the ward sister if I could put them in one cot so they could spend some time together. All the staff cried the day we put Hussein into Hassan's cot; it was amazing to watch how they immediately went back into the same position they had been in when they were joined. They looked at each other in wide-eyed wonder and gently stroked each other's faces, gurgling with such love and innocence. Eventually they fell asleep in that position and we dared not move them. Mr Kiely came into the room and took one look at them and said, 'Back together again, boys, where you belong!' I gazed down at my pair of angels and thought I had never seen anything as beautiful.

The hospital released a statement to the media. It said:

Twins Hassan and Hussein Benhaffaf left the intensive care unit at Great Ormond Street Hospital at the weekend and are now on a surgical ward. They are breathing unaided and are being bottle fed. Doctors at the hospital continue to be pleased by their progress and recovery. Earlier today, the boys were placed in the same cot together for the first time since they underwent separation surgery in April. Parents Angie and Azzedine Benhaffaf said:

'Our two little fighters have lived up to their name! We are happy to announce that Hassan and Hussein have left the intensive care unit and are doing well. We've enjoyed our first cuddles since their separation and they were worth the long wait. The boys were reunited for the first time today and it was very emotional to see them back together, in each other's arms. It feels just like a miracle and we cannot believe we got our happy ending. Thanks to everyone for your continued support. Their sisters Malika and Iman are getting used to their brothers being apart and are looking forward to holding each of the twins.'

A few days later we were told we could bottle feed the boys, which was incredible, and a couple of days later they were put on solids for the first time. I was so proud of them; I couldn't believe how quickly they were recovering. They were like an unstoppable life force. When the operations manager at the hospital, Ann Marie Kenneally, heard that they were going to be put on solids she bought some blue baby bowls and spoons for Hassan and got them in green for Hussein, to match their hospital colours. To this day I always feed Hassan with blue crockery and Hussein with green. With each passing day the boys got better and stronger and livelier and more beautiful. Sometimes I would have to pinch myself to make sure I was not dreaming. Mr Kiely was astounded at their progress; he said he couldn't really explain it, but I told him I believed all that prayer and positivity and hope they had received from people all over the world must have had something to do with it. They were defying all the odds; they were truly my Little Fighters.

One afternoon my phone rang and it was Heather Mills. The first time we had met her she promised me she would come and see the boys if their operation was a success; and, true to her word, she did come for a visit. Tearfully, I told her how I was desperately worried about my boys' futures; I thought because they had only one pelvis between them they might not be suitable for prosthetics. She told me not to worry and explained how it would work and reassured me that my boys would indeed walk and play and go on to live very full lives. She gave me such hope. I think she saw that day that we were completely drained by hospital life and had not seen anything but the inside of a ward for weeks. She very kindly offered to send a driver over for us so we could come to her house for a visit and the girls could play with her daughter Beatrice. Off we went for a couple of hours and spent a very enjoyable afternoon with her. She talked to our girls in a child-friendly way about prosthetics and how they worked; she told us that the important thing would be to get the right prosthetics for the boys, that their entire quality of life depended on it. I knew I would do everything in my power to make this a reality.

When Mr Kiely came to us a few days later and said the boys were almost ready to go home to Ireland we looked at him agog. We had been told they would be there for up to six months. It had been just six weeks since they were separated so we thought: 'Surely that can't be right!' We presumed he meant they would be transferred back to another hospital in Ireland. We could hardly believe our ears when he said, 'No, I mean home to your house. There is no reason for them to stay in hospital. They are too well to stay in a hospital any longer.' Azzedine and I were speechless; we just stood there looking at him while happiness rushed through us. 'I just can't explain it,' he said. 'I have never seen any other set of conjoined twins recover so quickly!' It was strange to hear a doctor with his experience say he couldn't explain why our babies had recovered so fast. I knew at that moment just how special our pair were. He told us the babies would be transferred to CUMH within days, not to be admitted as in-patients, but because the staff there could get to know them and their needs, and then we could go home! Azzedine and I just held each other and cried our eyes out; we could never in our wildest dreams have wished for this fairytale ending. I called Minister Martin to tell him we were coming home; he could not believe it either. This was May and I had organised for one of the Mums at Malika's school to pick up her schoolbooks for the following September, as we did not expect her to be back in time for the beginning of a new school year. Now we were looking at Malika returning to school before her summer holidays even started!

So, once again, and thankfully for the last time, a plan was put in place for us to go home to Cork. Azzedine said to me perhaps we should keep the fact that we were coming home quiet and just sneak in and not tell anybody, but there was no way I was sneaking around this time! The boys had been through so much, and under no circumstances would I be hiding them away. I was going to shout it at the top of my voice from every rooftop. I was going to tell the world that my Little Fighters were my heroes and they were coming home. This had been my dream from the very first time I found out the boys needed to be separated. I had imagined all six of us boarding a plane together, bound for home, hand in hand, triumphant, ready to begin our new lives. I remember thinking nothing could ever make me happier than for my boys to survive the operation and for all six of us to come home well, happy and together. When we had arrived home the previous December, everything was shrouded in grief; we were running around like fugitives in the night, a murky and uncertain future ahead of us. Now the boys were doing so well they were even baffling their own doctors. The world knew they were here and we didn't have to hide them any more. All I wanted to do now was try to rebuild our lives, get on with living like any normal family and watch our children grow up together.

The press office at GOSH told us that we needed to get a statement ready to release to the media that we were coming home. I pulled out a pen and paper and I just let what was in my joyous heart fall onto the paper. The statement read:

We are so relieved and so happy to announce that our little fighters are coming home tomorrow. All the prayers were answered and we thank God that it's all six of us returning home. Hassan and Hussein have gone through so much in their young lives already and now we hope that we can give them the happy future they both deserve. We again thank the public for their overwhelming love and support and the media for respecting our privacy and being so sensitive.

Thank you to the surgeons and staff at Great Ormond Street Hospital for giving our boys the incredible gift of separate lives! Not forgetting University College Hospital, London and Cork University Maternity Hospital who all shared in their care. As tough as the past year has been for all of us, we feel so much good has come out of this experience. Hassan and Hussein have brought out the best in everyone and reminded us all of the things that are important in life, which is family, unconditional love and above all hope.

Mr Edward Kiely, consultant paediatric surgeon at Great Ormond Street Hospital, said:

'The hospital is delighted that twins Hassan and Hussein Benhaffaf are in a position to return home to Ireland. We now have two very independent little boys with every chance of a great future.

'When the twins came into the operating theatre for separation they were joined from the chest to the pelvis. The operation itself turned out to be fairly straightforward. Their hearts were not joined, but nearly everything else was, that includes the liver, gut and bladder, all of which we separated. The boys also had one leg each, as that is how they were made. We have been very pleased with their recovery process and how they have thrived post separation. It is certainly not just down to me but to the whole team at the hospital who have provided the family with consistently high levels of care and expertise.'

The day before we were due to leave the hospital the HSE office in Cork asked us if they could put together a short statement about the boys coming home to Cork, as they were inundated with calls from the media. We agreed, but asked if they would put in an appeal for privacy, as after such a difficult eight weeks we were beaten down by exhaustion and just did not feel able for a barrage of calls and requests. What I wanted more than anything was to close my door, turn the lock and recover from what was the toughest year of our lives.

This is what was released the day of our return.

Following transfer from Great Ormond Street Children's Hospital in London today (Friday, 21 May 2010) the Health Service Executive can confirm that Hussein and Hassan Benhaffaf will be *cared for in the Paediatric Ward at Cork University Hospital. The medical teams in both hospitals have been liaising in advance of the boys' return to Ireland. The family has indicated that they would appreciate privacy on their return home. Consultant Paediatrician with Cork University Hospital, Deirdre Murray, said, 'Professor Hourihane and the CUH Paediatric Team have been liaising with the medical staff in Great Ormond Street regarding their care. We're delighted to hear that they have done very well following their surgery and we are looking forward to getting to know them. We also know that their parents are looking forward to spending some quiet time with them as a family after a difficult few months.'*

So on Friday, 21 May I woke at first light to such a sweet rush of happiness: we were going home! It was a gorgeous summer's morning and I could hear the roar of London outside. I lay in bed for a few moments and thought how truly happy I was to be returning to our quiet little village with its green fields and birdsong and peace. Although a statement had been released to say we were coming home, we hadn't given a time and we knew we would be picked up on the runway so we wouldn't be totally overwhelmed by the media. We were overcome with emotion as we said goodbye to the staff at GOSH; after all, they had been through this amazing journey with us every step of the way and felt like part of our family. Before we gathered up the boys' things we got some photographs taken with Mr Kiely and Prof Pierro, who held one of the boys each. I couldn't stop smiling as we packed for home.

As we boarded the same plane I had cried my eyes out in eight weeks earlier, I was delighted to notice the same pilot, Captain Mark Prendergast, was to bring us home. I cannot convey how utterly different that flight was to the last; now we were triumphant and in a party mood. There was laughter and jokes and singing and as we began our descent over Cork I took

Azzedine's hand and felt my heart soar with happiness. One of the Air Corps members told me there was a huge mob of media along the fence who would be able to see us as we got off the plane, but I said I didn't care. I wanted the world to see our boys and share in that magical moment when Azzedine and I stepped onto the runway with our sons. I had waited such a long time to get off a plane and feel happy and relaxed, and not eaten by worry. Azzedine got off with Hussein first and I followed with Hassan; I put my foot down on Irish soil with my wondrous boy in my arms. Malika skipped out onto the runway and the pilot carried my sleeping Iman. The media and well wishers started shouting, 'Welcome home, welcome home!' I felt emotion welling up from the pit of my stomach. I was so excited; I just started waving and punching the air and shouting, 'Up Cork and Up the rebels!' and 'They did it!' Malika shouted, 'Three cheers for the Little Fighters!' and we all laughed in delight. I looked around and Minister Martin was on the runway, standing in the same place where he had said goodbye to us just eight weeks earlier. Usually I would just shake his hand, but that day I threw my arms around him and gave him a kiss. It was our fairytale ending. I had dared to dream a dream and now I was living it.

When I look back now at the photographs and video footage of that day I can see a happiness in all of us I had believed I would never see again. In a later interview, Ryan Tubridy asked me what had been my happiest memory of the whole experience and I said it was the moment we touched down in Cork and got off the plane with our two boys in our arms. It was as if somebody had switched a light back on inside me.

An ambulance was waiting for us on the runway and a taxi for Azzedine and the girls. I climbed into the ambulance and the Gardaí escorted us all the way to the hospital from the airport. It felt as if we were in a movie as all the cars beeped and people excitedly waved at us as we passed. I thought I would explode I was so happy. We pulled up at the hospital to find the boys' new team waiting for us. I was so excited that I jumped off the ambulance and hugged and kissed all of them; I was literally bouncing with happiness. When we got to the boys' cubicle I noticed there were two cots for them; I asked the nurses if we could take one of the cots away as I wanted them to sleep together. I told them as long as I was alive they were never going to be apart again.

Later that evening I sat down with the boys to watch the 6 p.m. news, and I remember thinking I had rarely seen a more beautiful sight than our plane landing in Cork Airport; each of us getting off with a son and with our two daughters, and all those people waiting to meet us and share in our joy. I couldn't have imagined a happier ending. I kept thinking: 'Did all that really happen to us?' I was sitting there basking in the euphoria of it all when there was a gentle knock on the door; it was the Lord Mayor of Cork, Cllr Dara Murphy, and the Lady Mayoress, Tanya. They had brought with them two of the tiniest GAA Cork jerseys I had ever seen in my life; one read 'Hassan', the other 'Hussein'. It was such a lovely gesture. We immediately hung them over the boys' cot and chatted and took some photos. I was totally taken aback when the Lord Mayor told me they were planning a civic reception in honour of Hassan and Hussein! I told him I wanted it to be an open invitation event, so that everyone could come, but he said that just wasn't possible, but through him, as the people's representative, I would be able to thank the people of Cork. In my heart to this day I would have loved if every single person who had ever prayed or looked out for my boys could have come along, so I could personally thank each and every one of them. I always wonder if people ever truly knew just how much we appreciate every little thing they did for our sons. Whether it was a fundraiser, a quiet prayer or a card you sent—thank you—you helped us through the most difficult time of our lives.

Chapter 16 ～

| TEARS AND JOY

After five days we left the hospital and travelled home to Carrigtwohill. I couldn't wait to get in the door; throw open the windows, let the light into our home and enjoy the rest of the summer with my wonderful family around me. As we pulled into our little village, I noticed there were yellow ribbons and balloons tied to all the trees, covering everything. In days gone by, when war heroes returned, yellow ribbons symbolised a special welcome home for them. I quickly realised it was a special welcome home for us. It was lovely to think that our community had gone to so much trouble to welcome us back. The children in Malika's class had made a huge 'Welcome Home' banner, which hung outside the school—such a wonderful sight. I cried as we pulled up outside our house and I saw that people had hung loads of balloons and ribbons on our door. It meant a lot to me; all I had ever wanted since the boys' birth was a big welcome home for them and for there to be happiness and celebration and laughter. Finally I had my special moment and it had been so unexpected.

I brought the boys inside and put them in their cot, closed the door and just sat on the edge of the bed staring at them. I kept expecting to wake up and be back in that intensive care ward again, a place that haunted my every waking moment. I tried my best to get back to normal over the next few days, but I was plagued by my memories. It was as if a part of the trauma we had experienced in the hospital had crept into our baggage and come home with us. I would try to lie down for an hour when the boys were asleep, but all I could hear were those beeping monitors and those shrill alarms; I just couldn't switch them off in my head. I would often wake up in the middle of the night with a start, covered in sweat, and believe I was back there in that living nightmare. It was the same for Azzedine. It took at least a few weeks before we got over it. I knew we all desperately needed to recover from the enormous strain we had been under, so we turned off the phones for a while and concentrated on our own recovery as well as the boys'.

The twins settled in very well, as if they had never been away, and as exhausting as their care was I loved every moment of it. It wasn't long before they were keeping us up all night. Hassan in particular was very noisy; sometimes at about 4 a.m. he would suddenly start kicking his leg off the side of the cot over and over, which would wake Hussein and then he would start doing the same. They created the most unbelievable racket, but it was music to my ears. The boys then learned how to turn on their mobile in the middle of the night. I would suddenly wake up to the soothing sounds of Bach, Beethoven or Mozart and my boys beating their legs off their cot in time to the music! They were happy, always smiling, always laughing.

A couple of days after we returned home, Azzedine travelled up to Dublin to watch the Ireland versus Algeria soccer match with my brother-in-law, Alan. At first he didn't want to go as the kids were only home a few days, but I insisted. I knew he needed a break from it all. While he was travelling up I contacted Robin O'Sullivan to see if he knew anybody covering the match. He told me he knew the RTÉ sports journalist Tony O'Donoghue, so I asked him if there was any way it could be arranged for Azzedine to meet the Algerian team. I knew where Azzedine was sitting. Just before the match was due to start a startled Azzedine was brought down from his seat and introduced to the Algerian team and their manager. He also got to meet Giovanni Trapattoni, the Ireland manager. Later that night, as I was watching the 9 p.m. news with the girls, there was Azzedine hugging Trapattoni; we were whooping and screaming on the couch and desperately trying to find a tape to record it! Azzedine later told me that Trapattoni had said to him that when the boys grew up, maybe one of them could play for Ireland and one for Algeria! It made me very happy to watch Azzedine smiling and looking excited; it had been a long time since I'd seen my husband so relaxed and having fun.

———

Wednesday, 16 June was the day of the civic reception, and our house was alive with excitement. I decided it would be a good idea to dress the boys in the Cork jerseys the Lord Mayor had given to them, as, after all, this was a real Cork celebration! We were told we would be collected at 5.30 p.m. to be taken directly to the reception. I dressed the girls in gorgeous ivory dresses and managed to grab five minutes to get myself ready. I had been given a beautiful outfit by Sheena's Boutique in Cork especially for the occasion and, as I left my room to go and check on the boys, I touched the locket on my neck, a gift from Castle Jewellers, which I cherish to this day. It features my favourite photograph of the boys before they were separated and as I looked at it, I thought how far they had come and thanked my lucky stars for all our good fortune.

I was just about to go downstairs when I heard a roar of engines outside; there was beeping and the sound of people cheering and clapping. I had no idea what was going on, so I ran to the window to have a look. I couldn't believe it when I saw the huge motorcycles of the Rebel Riders Club and Two Wheel Training; just then an amazing white stretch limousine pulled into our estate. I called the girls to the window. I thought they would explode with excitement when they saw it. There was a knock on the door; it was John McCarthy and Johnny Chips of the Rebel Riders, who told me they were here to collect us and take us to the civic reception. It was so lovely I felt myself welling up with emotion immediately. We filed into the giant limo and were escorted all the way from Carrigtwohill to City Hall. When we looked out the front windscreen of the car, we saw that the bikers had formed an arrow and there were even more of them behind us. We went roaring through the village on that lazy sunny evening while everyone clapped and waved at us. It felt as if we were in a movie. We were all giddy and excited in the car; the girls loved it and I loved seeing them so happy. I was embarrassed every time they stopped the traffic to let us pass, as we were just a regular Mum and Dad with our kids, but it was such fun and a wonderful celebratory feeling, far removed from the last time we were home in Cork.

As we pulled up outside City Hall, I could see a big group of journalists and television cameras waiting for us to arrive. Robin had called me while we were in transit to let us know there was a significant media presence outside City Hall, so if we liked we could have sneaked in a back door, but I said no. We had done enough sneaking around; we were home now and this was our chance to thank everyone. I felt this was about sharing our joy and our boys with everyone. The local media had been incredibly supportive of us too, and I thought they deserved time to see the boys. We got out of the car on this beautiful summer's evening and saw a huge crowd of people and cameras flashing and everyone clapping and cheering. I held Hassan, and Azzedine held Hussein; it was a golden moment. Malika turned to me as we walked up the steps and said, 'Mummy, is this a dream?' I felt happy; it was our fairytale ending. The boys were home, the surgery was over, and we were all together starting out on our new life.

I looked around the room that day and saw that it was filled with people from all walks of life—old, young, rich, poor. There were doctors, nurses and journalists, Mums and Dads, business people, kids and bikers, all of whom had come together for the same reason—Hassan and Hussein. Pat O'Brien was there with his parents, and Mr Kiely and his wife Nicola. Mary Dinan came with her parents and everywhere I looked there were close friends and family. My father was there and Val was waving and all of Azzedine's friends from the Muslim community. People who had organised fantastic fundraisers for the kids were there along with neighbours and people from CUMH. I really would have loved to have invited everyone in the whole city, thrown open those doors to the people of Cork, but it just wasn't possible. I invited Adrian Walsh and the team from Fiat Ireland, as they had given us the use of a seven-seater van for a year, without which we could not get around as a family. The Lord Mayor said some amazing things about us as a family and I tried not to cry as I thanked everyone from the bottom of my heart. We went home that night and just basked in the loveliness of it all. We could hardly believe how we had come from a place of such sadness and fear to such joy and celebration in a few short weeks. The next morning we celebrated Iman's third birthday, just the six of us at home. I felt truly blessed.

The following weekend we packed up the family again and headed for Dublin to take part in Miriam O'Callaghan's chat show. It was her first show of the season and we were excited. I invited my friends Joan and Carmel to come with us. We returned to our friends at the Westbury Hotel and they were so happy to see us. Joseph, the manager, gave us the most fantastic suite and, as Iman had told him it had been her birthday the previous week, within an hour he had sent up an amazing birthday cake and lunch. RTÉ arranged for the girls and me to get our hair done, which was such a luxury, and soon it was time to set off for the show. We went upstairs to the Green Room where we met comedian Brendan O'Carroll and his wife Jenny, and I was very taken by them. They were sensitive and lovely in person. They told us they had followed the boys' story and how truly happy they were that they had done so well. They took my number and have kept in touch.

We were then introduced to Miriam; she was incredibly easy to talk to. The interview was very relaxed. I felt as if I were just chatting to someone in my own living room—it seemed all the more real as Iman decided to go walkabout in the studio! I was trying to keep one eye on Iman and the other on Miriam! Just as the interview was about to finish, Azzedine asked Miriam if he could say something. I was quite surprised and wondered what he was going to say; he said amazing things about me and how proud of me he was and how I had always put our children first. He is usually very shy and reserved. I was so proud of him!

The following morning was Father's Day and it was nice to have the whole family in Dublin for that special day. RTÉ organised for the children to get a VIP tour of Hamleys Toy Shop, where the girls were given two gorgeous fairy princess outfits as gifts and later we were brought to Dundrum Town Centre. I remember all these people crowding around us to see the twins and shake our hands. It was such a memorable day. Later we were taken to Nando's restaurant, where we had a lovely family meal together—we felt very spoiled. We had been through hardship and pain; it felt good to put our worries somewhere else for a few hours.

Just a few days after we returned home to Cork we were treated to a very special homecoming celebration by our local community in Carrigtwohill. Everyone from the village showed up and we were transported to our local community centre in a vintage car. It was much more low-key than the city reception, which was perfect for us. It was so heart-warming to see everyone around us celebrating the boys. One of my neighbours, Billy, sang Michael Jackson's 'You Are Not Alone' accompanied by her two children, which made me incredibly emotional. The Rebel Riders came and presented the boys with a special hat each. It was a heady summer's evening with the smell of freshly cut grass in the air. Everybody was dressed in their summer clothes and the girls ran about with excitement. We were overjoyed to be reunited with our friends and neighbours in such happy circumstances. As I climbed into bed that night I thought how different life would be if the boys hadn't been so lucky.

——

Little by little things started to get back to normal. We would take the kids to the park and do the grocery shopping, and all these everyday things filled me with joy and happiness. At night I would put the boys in their cot, top to tail, as now they were too big to sleep side by side, and every single morning they would be back shoulder to shoulder again. I loved it. I would say to them every morning, 'Back together again, boys!' and they would giggle and kick their legs and beam up at me with those smiles that would melt the hardest of hearts.

The anniversary of when we had first found out that the boys were conjoined loomed and I was dreading it. I didn't want to look back now that we had come so far, but as it drew near all the things we had been through since that fateful day started to play around in my mind, filling me with sadness. I couldn't help reminiscing and thinking back to how 12 months previously I had been very happy to be expecting another child and how everything had changed utterly on that that black day when a land mine exploded in our lives, shattering our little family.

A year to the day of that unhappy event I woke to the sound of the phone ringing just before 7 a.m. I remember being quite startled by it. Azzedine picked up the phone; it was his brother in Algeria. I saw my husband's expression change; his brother had called to tell him his mother had died. Azzedine dropped the phone, devastated. I held him as he cried like a child; he had adored his mother and it tore him apart that he had not seen her before she died. He had such love and respect for her. He was the youngest of 10 and was the baby of the family. In the past we had always gone to Algeria in the summer with the girls, but we had not been able to travel over the previous 12 months because I had fallen pregnant and then obviously we couldn't go anywhere once the twins were born.

I immediately went online to try to buy him a ticket to get him home, but he could not find his Algerian passport anywhere; we tore the house apart. I booked a flight to London so he could pick up a visa there for Algeria, but then we realised all the flights to Algeria out of London were booked out for that weekend. He couldn't get a flight until the following Monday from Dublin. By the time he got there his poor mother had been buried. It was extremely difficult for him.

While Azzedine was in London, Hassan started throwing up quite violently; he just couldn't keep anything down. After about an hour of this I began to get very concerned about him, so I called our GP, Dr Mary Barry. She told me Hassan looked very dehydrated and would need to go to hospital. I was on my own with the four children and I was upset and scared. Later that day, when Azzedine returned from London, I brought Hassan to CUH. He was there until Sunday and we were relieved that we could take him home before Azzedine left for Algeria. Val agreed to come and stay with me for the week and I said a tearful goodbye to my grieving husband.

I woke up in the middle of the night to the sound of Hassan's weak cries. He was vomiting and his eyes looked so sunken they frightened me. He was highly unresponsive; I rang the hospital and they sent an ambulance for him. I couldn't believe it—my husband had just left the country and I was back in an ambulance again with one of my sons. I was hysterical. I felt very alone in the hospital, alone and scared. We were admitted to a ward and I was told Hassan had Adenovirus and was very unwell. He had lost a lot of weight and looked lifeless and tiny. He had always been my little chubby, healthy-looking boy; now he looked gaunt, ill, a shadow of the bouncing baby he'd been a few days before. It broke my heart to see him like that.

I could hardly believe I was back in a hospital standing over my son attached to drips and nose tubes. I never wanted to be surrounded by all that paraphernalia of fear again. I hated that hospital smell and the bright lights and the fear that lives in children's wards. We were supposed to be going forward not backwards! The situation kept getting worse as the following Tuesday Hussein started to vomit and he ended up in the same cot as his brother at the hospital. Azzedine was distraught when I told him. I tried to play it down as much as I could, but I knew he was desperately worried. It was such a difficult week; I was going back and forth between the girls and the hospital. I was exhausted and one night I realised with terror that I had fallen asleep at the wheel on my way home.

The boys remained in the hospital for 18 days and were very unwell and weak. I felt sorry that the girls were stuck in the house again while they were supposed to be enjoying their summer holidays. Azzedine returned five days later, on Friday, 9 July. I went from the hospital to pick him up and I remember running into his arms in the airport; holding him and crying. I was never so happy to see him in my life. Lots of people at the airport recognised us and came to ask how the boys were doing; it took all my strength just to hold back my tears and smile and nod. Finally on 14 July Hussein was allowed home. I found it very hard to part my boys; I always felt that at least when they were together they would have each other no matter what happened, but thankfully on Monday, 19 July, Hassan was allowed home and we were all back together again.

| ONE YEAR ON

In August the boys had their first appointment with Enable Ireland, a centre that works with children with a wide spectrum of disabilities. I had been dreading the appointment because at that stage I was still finding it difficult to accept that my boys had a disability. I arrived at the centre full of confidence, feeling very protective of my sons. I was worried about what they would say to me about my boys' futures; I didn't feel ready to hear that my sons might not be able to do all the things that other children could do. I met with the centre's senior physiotherapist, Gillian O'Dywer, an occupational therapist and a social worker. We sat down to discuss Hassan and Hussein and I told them everything that the boys had been through up to that point. I was full of pride in my sons' abilities. I wanted people to see them through my proud mother's eyes: I saw only their abilities, not their disabilities. I had never liked having to introduce them to new medical professionals all over again, trying to convince people that they were not sick babies but healthy, strong and happy.

After the introductions were over I was asked to undress the boys down to their vests and lie them on an exercise mat so that Gillian could assess them. I felt then, because I was their Mum, that I had to put on a positive front for my children. I tried my best to be strong that day, but when I saw my two little boys with their dancing eyes stripped down to their vests lying on that mat, their disability was staring me in the face—I could ignore it no longer. I looked at their smiling little faces and burst out crying. I was aware that I had said in interviews that the boys would not only do what every other child could do, but would do it better. That was how I had thought at the time. I realised I had to face the fact that there were things that my boys might never be able to do. It broke my heart that day as I finally began to accept that no matter how I looked at it, they had a disability and a pretty significant one at that. I had to acknowledge that even though I thought they were perfect, the fact was they were missing limbs, and that meant the road ahead was always going to be a hard one. I cried my heart out as I admitted to the staff that I was terrified and didn't understand how my babies were ever going to crawl or move or walk when they couldn't even sit up by themselves.

I cannot convey how amazing the staff at Enable Ireland have been to Azzedine and me as parents and of course to my boys, since that initial appointment. It was their first time catering for babies with their particular needs, so it was also quite a challenge for them too, but I know they are doing everything in their power to help my precious pair. With Enable Ireland I can just be myself. I don't have to put on a front or pretend everything is all right, or be positive all the time; I feel I can just go there and if I am feeling distraught or have had a bad day, I can be honest with them about it. They are incredible. If I could have one wish granted it would be to build them a huge, state-of-the-art centre, so they would have everything they could possibly need to carry out their fantastic work. They put a plan in place for the boys straight away and it's still ongoing to this day. The twins do three hourly physiotherapy and occupational therapy sessions there up to three times a week and we do a series of exercises with them every day at home.

The staff at the facility have helped me to accept that we have a very long road ahead of us with the boys; their care is for life. Their disability is not something that is suddenly going to get better, or just eventually fix itself. This has been one of the most difficult things I have had to accept about my sons. Obviously you want the best of everything for your children; you never want them to suffer or miss out, or be held back in any way. Sometimes I feel so incredibly sad when I think how they could suffer as they are growing up, but I know all you can do as a Mum is your best to make it better for them. I will get them the best prosthetics I can, and do everything in my power to give them a normal, happy life. I know, no matter what they need, I will get it for them—somehow. They deserve the best of everything; nobody has ever fought as hard for life as those two boys.

Malika returned to school at the end of August and little Iman began Montessori. With both girls out for a few hours most days, Azzedine and I began to attend the boys' many and varied appointments together. I also took great pleasure in simply doing the everyday things with my sons, such as bringing them to the Go Safari play centre in Carrigtwohill or to the park. My friend Betty had a baby boy the week after the twins were born so Hassan and Hussein enjoyed many playdates with their little friend Gerry! Some of our friends and neighbours have remained a great support, but I was struck by how few people have called to see us since the boys' separation. When the babies were joined, we had many visitors and well wishers—the house was always full of people, and I loved that, but little by little it began to dry up after the surgery. People stopped calling by although the awful thing was it was then that we needed them the most. When I was pregnant I felt desperately alone; very few people had looked out for me and sadly, during the months after we returned home following the boys' separation, I began to feel that I was back in that lonely place again, on my own, and it broke my heart. It would be so fantastic to have the level of support that we require to enable Azzedine to return to work, but it's just not possible as the boys need such a high level of hands-on care.

In late September I got the boys ready to attend the launch of an awards ceremony very close to home: the Cork Person of the Year Awards at the Silversprings Moran Hotel in Cork. I was going to dress them up in their little suits, but then I thought what could be more fitting than their matching Cork City FC jerseys, which had been gifted to them by the manager of Fota Wildlife Park! There was a lovely atmosphere at the event that night; people said the boys were an inspiration and afterwards crowded around us to get their photographs taken with them. I was so proud of my little happy sons. I was told they were to receive The Hope for the Future award, which I felt was fitting because that is what they are and will always be—the living embodiment of hope. The following day the *Evening Echo* ran a large front page picture of the boys with the headline 'Look at Us Now!' I loved it; it was such a happy picture and a chance for the people of Cork who had followed the boys' story to see how they were thriving.

October arrived and I was asked to launch National Breastfeeding Week by the Friends of Breastfeeding group, as I was a well-known Mum and they were aware I was very passionate about breastfeeding. It felt great to do something that was just about me and to talk about something I was greatly interested in. I shared my own experiences about how I had breastfed the girls until they were two years old, but I also told how difficult it had been to breastfeed the boys in the early days before my milk dried up. I compared it with a game of Twister, which drew some chuckles from the crowd! I talked about how perseverance was key when it came to breastfeeding, and encouraged other Mums not to give up.

In mid-October we were told we would have to go back to London for a check-up in November. I was filled with trepidation as I booked the flights—I knew first-hand how unpredictable these tests could be. I had gone to that hospital in the past, full of confidence, and been given life-changing and devastating news.

This time I was going to be a lot more cautious. Even though the boys seemed to be thriving, I had learned not to be overly optimistic. When the ITN film crew contacted us a few days later proposing we make a follow-up documentary, at first I thought it might be too much to take on so soon, but when they told us that people were very eager to see how the twins were doing, after some consideration we agreed. I was very aware the first documentary had been quite painful viewing; now I was happy to let people see how well the boys were doing now. I wanted to share their first birthday too and give back some of the happiness to all those people who had taken the time to help and support us.

That same week the boys attended the Cork Person of the Year event to accept their award. They had been very sociable during the night—I had brought them from table to table and they were kissing and hugging and babbling at getting their photographs taken with everyone—but then, just 10 minutes before their award, they fell fast asleep, so I had to accept it on their behalf. The very next day was quite an emotional one too as the boys had an appointment at Enable Ireland to try out their first ever sitting prosthetic, which had been moulded to fit their shape. We had no idea what to expect when we arrived at Enable Ireland that afternoon. We were shown these little static structures that the boys would be placed in and would wear for a few hours every day. The prosthetic would help them to keep their spines straight and teach them to sit up straight and not at an angle. Hussein was put in his first and then placed in a baby chair. I really hadn't expected to feel emotional about it, but when I looked at him in his prosthetic, he just seemed so small and vulnerable that I burst out crying. It really came home to me that day that this was just the first baby step in an enormous lifelong challenge for my sons. I was holding Hassan in my arms at the time and I had to hand him over to Azzedine and run out of the room to compose myself. Gillian had been explaining to us how everything, from the way they sit up to the way they crawl to the way we hold them in our arms, would have to be done a certain way; other children just sit up and crawl and it all comes naturally, but with our boys everything would have to be done in stages. She told us if we put in a big effort during the first five years of their lives, making sure they got the right amount of care to straighten their posture and ensuring they were elongated at all times, they would have a good chance of walking as well as possible with a prosthetic limb in future—but, if not, the opportunity would be lost forever. We knew we had our work cut out for us, especially as we had not only one child with a disability, but two.

A couple of weeks later when I returned home from shopping, I found Azzedine had put the boys in each of their sitting prosthetics and placed an activity table between them. I couldn't believe how great they looked when I walked in and found them sitting up and playing away like any other set of twins. In the evenings Azzedine and I would do the boys' physiotherapy at home and let the girls join in, which they loved. Little by little we got used to our new way of life. One day while I was playing with the boys on the rug, I suddenly noticed Hassan had started to crawl along on his belly. I held my breath, afraid to move, hoping that Azzedine would come into the room. It wasn't long before the two boys were proudly sitting up on their own. The joy it gave us to see them moving about independently convinced us that separating them had been the right decision. Their physiotherapist was surprised by how quickly they had begun to crawl and by how determined they were to move about, despite everything, but I knew they were my Little Fighters! I would just sit and stare at my bright-eyed boys, sitting up and looking back at me with their toothy grins, clapping and reaching for their sisters, and thank God for those surgeons and the wonderful team at GOSH.

In November, we travelled up to the Shelbourne Hotel in Dublin to attend the Maternity and Infant Awards. They had decided to honour us as a family with a special merit award for the courage and bravery we had shown during the boys' incredible first year! We were very excited. Natalie and Dave from ITN started the first day of filming at the event and we met some truly inspirational people. When it came to our award, which was the last one of the day, a huge screen dropped down and a beautiful collage of photographs was displayed while a voiceover read out the poem I had composed for my sons. It was a very emotional experience, and there wasn't a dry eye in the house. When the introductions were over we got up to accept the award, and everyone in the room got to their feet and clapped. I was completely overwhelmed by people's kindness; I kept thinking if somebody had told me 12 months previously that we would be accepting an award and getting a standing ovation from hundreds of people, I would have told them they were dreaming; now I was the one who felt I was in a dream.

As soon as we got home from Dublin and unpacked the suitcase, we had to pack it again for London. As nervous as I was about the boys' tests, I was most excited to pick up their passports for the first time; they had never needed them before because they had always flown with the Air Corps. As I handed over our bags at the check-in desk, I was transported back to the last time I had checked in for an Aer Lingus flight. I shuddered when I recalled just how frightened we had been and how uncertain our futures were. This time everybody was chatting to us on the flight and asking to see the boys, and the air hostesses kept bringing down sweets for the girls; they spoiled us rotten!

The following day the boys were admitted for tests and we had some nail-biting hours waiting for their results, but the staff were more than happy with their progress—everything looked great. I brought them back to the Woodland Ward and the PICU ward to visit the staff there and they were so happy to see them; it was a lovely reunion. With the film crew at our sides we went back to the theatre where the boys had been separated to meet some of the surgeons. It felt surreal walking back down that awful corridor, Azzedine holding Hassan while I held Hussein. Later that day, I met Mr Kiely to go through the boys' test results; we met in the

exact same room where one year previously I had been told about
the boys' missing limbs. It was very difficult to go back into that
place where my heart had been smashed into a million pieces and
my hopes for my boys had temporarily died, but thankfully this
time it was all good news.

The following day we visited Winter Wonderland in London
with the children and brought the twins to see Santa Claus for the
first time—Hassan bawled his eyes out while Hussein tried to pull
Santa's beard off—we all laughed hard. I had never felt happier.

We returned to Cork and looked forward to celebrating the
twins' first birthday the following week, but not before the boys
were invited to switch on Cork City's Christmas lights! I was
excited to get such a lovely and meaningful invitation from our
city. The people at Cork City Council told us they thought the
twins had brought so much light into the lives of the people of
Cork that it was only fitting they be the ones to officially begin the
season of light. I remember how cold it was on that podium but
the warmth and love coming from the people of Cork was
overwhelming. As it was the twins' birthday in just a few short
days, the MC asked the whole crowd to sing 'Happy Birthday' to
them. There was a brass band behind us playing along and it was
a fantastic moment. I felt incredibly emotional and couldn't hold
back my tears. I was happy that these people, who had been
extremely supportive of us all along, were there to celebrate this
special moment with us.

A few days later we decided to bring the kids to Fota Island in
East Cork for a special treat. We took the kid's train around the
island. Malika and Iman tried to catch snowflakes on their
tongues while the boys laughed and gurgled, all wrapped up in
their winter coats and hats, kicking their legs with excitement. It
was a magical day.

On Thursday, 2 December, we celebrated Hassan and Hussein's
first birthday: a real milestone. The twins were born at 10.21 a.m. so
at that exact time Azzedine and I were on Youghal Beach with our

amazing sons. When we had brought the boys to the beach back in March, it had been my wish that we would return with them when they had been separated, so they could breathe in the sea air, listen to the waves breaking on the shore and watch the seagulls soar free in the sky. It was an emotional moment. When we pulled up at the beach I remember Azzedine shouted, 'Freedom!' and we knew that one day soon we would be bringing them back here and watching them swim in the sea with their sisters, and building sand castles in the sun. When the girls finished school that day we held a private party at home, just the six of us, exchanging presents and enjoying each other's company. We went out to Mahon Point, our local shopping centre, and loads of people came over to say 'Happy Birthday' to the twins.

As we were leaving the shopping centre, out of the corner of my eye I caught a glimpse of the kiosk I had visited the previous November when I was pregnant with the boys. I had to go over! It was manned by the very same girl who had been there the previous year. 'I remember you!' she said and told me how she recalled how upset I had been the year before and how afterwards she had seen me on the news and had understood why I had been so sad. I decided to buy another tree decoration from her, this time with six little characters on which I had all our names engraved. It was the perfect ending to a perfect day.

Two days later we held the twins' very special first birthday party. It had been such a horribly cold week—it seemed as if the whole of east Cork had turned into an ice rink! I was worried that people would not make it to the celebrations, but Mr Kiely and Mr Peter Kuckow thankfully managed to fly in from the UK and make it down to us in the ice and the snow. Sharon Poleon, who had made the boys' cake for their naming party, offered to make a very special and unique first birthday cake for them, which was two-tiered and in the shape of an octagon. On each side was a photograph representing a different stage of the boys' journey throughout the previous year. It was absolutely incredible. I dressed the girls up in matching red dresses and the boys in shirts and ties and we headed to the Go Safari centre. We cut the cake and everybody in the room sang 'Happy Birthday' to my sons as the documentary crew filmed. I was tearful looking at my little boys, only one year old and already they had been through so much. To look at their happy faces and their dancing eyes you would never guess how much they had endured. It was the perfect day I had hoped it would be, full of joy and laughter and celebration.

Soon Christmas began to draw near and I remember being struck by how different it felt that year. Our boys were home, the six of us were alive and well and the future seemed full of possibility and light again. There were smiles and laughter in our home now, not tears and anguish. We had waved goodbye to hospitals, intensive care wards and ambulances. The boys were doing well, and although we knew they still had an uphill battle ahead of them, we were ready to face it together. The kids went to bed early on Christmas Eve and the following morning awoke to find Santa had left presents for four very special children. We hung the new Christmas decoration on the tree as the boys gurgled and laughed at its twinkling light. The six of us had a special day, wanting nothing more than to be together, watching family movies. Azzedine and I reminisced over dinner about the terrible year it had been and discussed our fledgling hopes for the future—just like old times.

That night, as I tucked my four wonderful children into bed, I thanked God for blessing me with so much. I tiptoed away from my sleeping boys' cot and paused for a moment before turning off the light. I realised I had everything I could ever want. The boys had been a gift and now I could look forward to the coming year without fear and uncertainty. I could live again and hold the dream of seeing my beautiful boys walk hand in hand together some day in my heart. After all, I knew that miracles still happen and dreams do come true.

ACKNOWLEDGMENTS

Thanks to my husband Azzedine and my children, Malika, Iman, Hassan and Hussein. You have made my life complete.

I would like to thank my father, my Aunt Val and Sinead Devine who helped us through our really difficult pregnancy and birth. The care that I was given at CUMH by Dr Keelin O'Donoghue, Marian Cunningham and Margo Fenton was exceptional. My GPs, Dr Mary Barry and Dr Lynda O'Callaghan, went beyond the call of duty in their care for me. I must especially thank Micheál Martin TD for helping us through the birth, separation and homecoming for the boys. Also the Irish Air Corps, Cork Airport, the HSE and Tony McCullagh.

At UCLH thanks to Mae Nugent, Mary Dinan and Kati Grey for your kindness, friendship and help. Thanks to Mr Pat O'Brien, my obstetrician, who was so supportive, along with all his team at UCLH, Pran, Mark, Bev, Mary and all the wonderful midwives who looked after me so well.

I will never truly be able to express my gratitude to all at NICU, PICU and Woodland Ward in GOSH for their care of Hassan and Hussein. We were blessed to have Mr Edward Kiely, a fellow Corkman, as well as Prof Pierro and Mr Peter Kuckow. Thanks to everyone who worked through the day and night of the twins' separation and to Erica and Yan. Also Ellie, Mark and Laura, and the chaplains especially Abu, Fatima, Penny and Sr Catherine. Special thanks to Jo, Stephen and Hayley at GOSH Press Office for all your help and guidance. Also Anne-Marie Conneally for being so supportive, and Carmita and all at Weston House for their genuine care.

I want to thank everyone at CUMH for your help and support. Thanks to Dr Filan, Kannan, Anne Buckley, Sheila, Lucille, Anne Twomey, and everyone at Neo. Also Rebecca for your breastfeeding support! Thanks to Angie O'Brien and the HSE Press Office for your help and guidance. And at CUH, Tir Na nOg Ward and the Childrens Club.

Thanks to Robin O'Sullivan, 'my security blanket'! We will always be grateful to you.

Thanks to my friends and neighbours Alex and Betty for your continuous support.

For those of you who organised or supported a fundraiser, thank you. Special thanks to John Mac, Johnny Chips, Jason and all the Rebel Riders, Two Wheel Training and all the participants in the Twins Bike Run 2010 and to RedFM.

Thank you to Adrian Walsh and the team at Fiat Ireland for the loan of a van which enabled us to travel together as a family.

Thanks to Enable Ireland, Cork for the boys' ongoing care. We are truly grateful. Also thanks to Pat Kiely and Mike Fuohy.

Thanks, Tom and Helen, for taking our little Buddy.

Thanks to everyone who prayed, sent a card or supported us in any way. We deeply appreciated your help. We would also like to thank Ambulance Service; Babyscan Ltd; Brehon Hotel; Captain Americas—Ronnie Delaney; Julie Callanan; Carmel Bourke and Joan Scully; Carrigtwohill community and school; Carrigtwohill Pharmacy; ChildAid; all the children who made cards; Christian and Muslim communities; Cork City Council; Cork County Council; Cork Multiples Club; D Hotel; Debenhams; Sarah Delaney (DFA); Dr Joe Dillon; Dingle Skellig Hotel; Gerry Dwyer, HSE; EBS… for being patient!; Evening Echo; Exclusive PR—Amanda Stocks and Rebecca Smith; Facebook friends; Ford Ireland; Fota Wildlife Park; Marisa Fragolini; Dr Orla Franklin; Friends of Breastfeeding; Glanmire Crochet Group; Go Safari Playcentre; Hamleys Toyshop Dundrum; Mary and Liam Holton; INEC; Infant and Maternity Awards; Irish Examiner; Irish Multiple Births Association; ITN—Natalie Fay, Dave Harman, Julie Etchingham; Charlotte Kamel; Alice Kearney; Marie Kiernan; Lee Motorcycles; President and Dr McAleese and staff at the Áras; McCarthy family; Cllr Laura McGonigle; Clodagh McKenna; all media; Heather Mills; Mothercare; John Mullins at Bord Gáis Energy; Caroline Murphy, RTÉ; Dara and Tanya Murphy; Nandos—Beverley Swift; Brendan and Jenny O'Carroll; Patricia O'Neill; Vincent O'Neill; Elaine and Nicola O'Sullivan; Permanent TSB Patrick Street, Cork—Aeneas Lane; Sharon Poleon; Provision; REHAB People of the Year Awards; Angela Roche at Babybiz; RTÉ; the late Gerry Ryan; Salih family; Paschal Sheehy, RTÉ; SMA; Smyths Toystore—John Keenan; Source SilverSprings; SuperValu; Treatment Abroad Office; Ryan Tubridy; Noreen Tully; Vodafone—Anne O'Leary; Wiser Bins.

I want to thank Edel O'Connell for sharing this amazing journey with me. We laughed and we cried writing this book but it was an unforgettable experience! Thanks to Fergal Tobin for believing I had a 'book in me' and the Gill & Macmillan team for all their tremendous support.

Azzedine and I would like to offer our full support and care to anyone who goes through the experience of having conjoined twins in the future. Please feel free to contact us through any of the three hospitals that shared in our care:

Cork University Maternity Hospital —Cork
University College London Hospital—London
Great Ormond Street Hospital—London

Twins—Double the Trouble, but Twice the Love!

If you would like to donate to help with Hassan and Hussein's ongoing care, you can do so at:

The Little Fighters Fund
Permanent TSB
Patrick Street
Cork

Sort Code: 99-07-03
Account: 16556196